*

To Isa and our two children

– Dr. Dominik Hauser

Contributors

About the author

Dr. Dominik Hauser is an iOS developer working for a small company in western Germany. In over 11 years as an iOS developer, he has worked on many different apps, both large and small. In his spare time, Dominik builds small (often silly) apps and explores how he can become a better iOS developer. He talks at conferences, writes books, and is active in the iOS community in general. His most successful open source component (in terms of stars) is a *pull-to-refresh control* for a table view that consists of an actual SpriteKit game.

Before Dominik became an iOS developer, he was a physicist, researching the most powerful photon sources within our galaxy.

Thank you, Isa, for your continued support, patience, and encouragement.

Test-Driven iOS Development with Swift

Fourth Edition

Write maintainable, flexible, and extensible code using the power of TDD with Swift 5.5

Dr. Dominik Hauser

BIRMINGHAM—MUMBAI

Test-Driven iOS Development with Swift
Fourth Edition

Group Product Manager: Rohit Rajkumar
Publishing Product Manager: Ashitosh Gupta
Senior Editor: Keagan Carneiro
Content Development Editor: Adrija Mitra
Technical Editor: Joseph Aloocaran
Copy Editor: Safis Editing
Project Coordinator: Rashika Ba
Proofreader: Safis Editing
Indexer: Pratik Shirodkar
Production Designer: Roshan Kawale
Marketing Coordinator: Elizabeth Varghese

First published: February 2016
Second edition: October 2016
Third edition: October 2017
Fourth edition: March 2022

Production reference: 3060522

Published by Packt Publishing Ltd.
Livery Place
35 Livery Street
Birmingham
B3 2PB, UK.

978-1-80323-248-5
www.packt.com

About the reviewers

Nour Araar is a software engineer with extensive experience in mobile and web development who has built many medium- to large-scale apps, and who also has interests in AI/ML, data science, cloud solutions, and competitive programming. He has participated in many competitions not only as a contestant but also as a coach, and has also worked as a teaching assistant in university after graduating as an AI engineer. He loves to share his experience, and his motto is, everyone should learn to code and become a programmer, which is why he makes videos and writes blogs helping others to learn how to code, on YouTube and Medium, as well as on his own website.

Kenneth Michael Dubroff is a single dad and experienced iOS developer. He currently works with several talented iOS and Android developers, managing releases for the adaptive fitness app JRNY. He also works as a tech editor for the server-side Swift team at raywenderlich.com. Kenny also recently finished editing a book with *raywenderlich. com* entitled *Real-World iOS*, which focuses on best practices for mid-level developers. Kenny previously assisted various private clients through freelance contracts, sometimes managing apps from start to release, sometimes adding new features, and always wanting to refactor.

> *I would like to thank my daughter, son, dad, and grandparents. None of my accomplishments would be possible without your past and continued support!*

> *It was a pleasure editing Test-Driven iOS Development with Swift. The team put in a lot of hard work and I hope you find it as insightful as I have!*

Table of Contents

3

Test-Driven Development in Xcode

Section 2 – The Data Model

4

The App We Are Going to Build

5

Building a Structure for ToDo Items

6

Testing, Loading, and Saving Data

Section 3 – Views and View Controllers

7

Building a Table View Controller for the To-Do Items

8
Building a Simple Detail View

9
Test-Driven Input View in SwiftUI

Section 4 – Networking and Navigation

10
Testing Networking Code

11
Easy Navigation with Coordinators

Index

Other Books You May Enjoy

Preface

Automatic tests are an essential part of agile software development, especially unit tests, with their quick and reliable feedback helping developers to keep projects maintainable and clean. **Test-driven development** (**TDD**) methodology gives developers clear rules about how to build scalable, maintainable, and – as such – agile projects. Often, once the initial aversion to writing tests before the code is overcome, developers stick to TDD because they feel that their code is better and they are more confident in the result.

In this book, we will explore how to write unit tests for many different aspects of iOS development for iOS 15+. All that will be done in the context of test-driven development. The book starts with an introduction to testing in general and TDD in iOS apps and continues with building a complete app throughout the book. It covers basic UI structures, the Combine framework, async/await, and even SwiftUI.

After you've worked through the book and challenged yourself in the exercises, you will be able to write tests for a variety of code in iOS development, and you will have the tools to decide what to learn next in your journey to become an expert in test-driven iOS development.

Who this book is for

TDD is a proven way to find software bugs early. Writing tests before you code improves the structure and maintainability of your apps. This book will guide you through the steps for creating a complete app using TDD and cover the core elements of iOS apps: view controllers, views, navigation, networking, Combine, and SwiftUI.

If you have already made your first small iOS apps and want to learn how to improve your work using automated unit tests, then this book is for you.

What this book covers

Chapter 1, *Your First Unit Tests*, sees the first unit tests at work. We write real tests for a fictional blogging app and explore the different kinds of assertions in XCTest, a testing framework from Apple.

Chapter 2, Understanding Test-Driven Development, looks at test-driven development and how it can help us developers to write maintainable code.

Chapter 3, Test-Driven Development in Xcode, brings the insights from the first two chapters together and looks at how test-driven development works in Xcode. You'll learn some tricks and configurations that make Xcode a valuable testing tool.

Chapter 4, The App We Are Going To Build, discusses the app we are going to build in the rest of the book. This chapter ends with setting up the project for the app in Xcode.

Chapter 5, Building a Structure for ToDo Items, shows how to build the model layer of our app. By working on it, you will learn how to write tests for Combine code.

Chapter 6, Testing, Loading, and Saving Data, addresses the fact that the data used in the app needs to be saved and loaded in the file system of the iOS device. In this chapter, we build the class that is responsible for this task.

Chapter 7, Building a Table View Controller for the To-Do Items, shows how to write tests for a table view with a diffable data source. You will learn how to test updates of table view cells and the selection of cells.

Chapter 8, Building a Simple Detail View, explores how to test user interface elements such as labels, buttons, and maps. We also take a look at how to test actions of the user that change the data in the model layer.

Chapter 9, Test-Driven Input View in SwiftUI, shows how to build and test a view created using SwiftUI. In order to be able to test SwiftUI code, we add a third-party testing library to the testing target.

Chapter 10, Testing Networking Code, looks at writing tests for the new async/await APIs of URLSession. This will allow you to write clean tests that simulate the network communication with a fast mock object.

Chapter 11, Easy Navigation with Coordinators, the final chapter, shows how to write tests for navigation between the view controllers of our app. This allows us, finally, to see our small app running on the simulator. We fix the last bugs using TDD and end up with a working app.

To get the most out of this book

You need the latest version of Xcode installed on your Mac. The code in this book has been tested with Xcode 13 and Swift 5.5 but it should also work with newer versions of Xcode and Swift.

Software/hardware covered in the book	Operating system requirements
Xcode 13, Swift 5.5	macOS

If you are using the digital version of this book, we advise you to type the code yourself or access the code from the book's GitHub repository (a link is available in the next section). Doing so will help you avoid any potential errors related to the copying and pasting of code.

You should try to do all the exercises in the book. They are designed to give you more insight and strengthen your experience.

Download the example code files

You can download the example code files for this book from GitHub at https://github.com/PacktPublishing/Test-Driven-iOS-Development-with-Swift-Fourth-Edition. If there's an update to the code, it will be updated in the GitHub repository.

We also have other code bundles from our rich catalog of books and videos available at https://github.com/PacktPublishing/. Check them out!

Download the color images

We also provide a PDF file that has color images of the screenshots and diagrams used in this book. You can download it here: http:https://static.packt-cdn.com/downloads/9781803232485_ColorImages.pdf.

Conventions used

There are a number of text conventions used throughout this book.

Code in text: Indicates code words in text, database table names, folder names, filenames, file extensions, pathnames, dummy URLs, user input, and Twitter handles. Here is an example: "A table view is usually represented by UITableViewController, which is also the data source and delegate for the table view."

A block of code is set as follows:

```
// APIClient.swift
lazy var geoCoder: GeoCoderProtocol
    = CLGeocoder()
```

When we wish to draw your attention to a particular part of a code block, the relevant lines or items are set in bold:

```
mkdir src/client/apollo
touch src/client/apollo/index.js
```

Bold: Indicates a new term, an important word, or words that you see onscreen. For instance, words in menus or dialog boxes appear in **bold**. Here is an example: "From the **Details** screen, the user will be able to check an item."

Tips or Important Notes
Appear like this.

Get in touch

Feedback from our readers is always welcome.

General feedback: If you have questions about any aspect of this book, email us at customercare@packtpub.com and mention the book title in the subject of your message.

Errata: Although we have taken every care to ensure the accuracy of our content, mistakes do happen. If you have found a mistake in this book, we would be grateful if you would report this to us. Please visit www.packtpub.com/support/errata and fill in the form.

Piracy: If you come across any illegal copies of our works in any form on the internet, we would be grateful if you would provide us with the location address or website name. Please contact us at copyright@packt.com with a link to the material.

If you are interested in becoming an author: If there is a topic that you have expertise in and you are interested in either writing or contributing to a book, please visit authors.packtpub.com.

Share Your Thoughts

Once you've read *Test-Driven iOS Development with Swift* Fourth Edition, we'd love to hear your thoughts! Scan the QR code below to go straight to the Amazon review page for this book and share your feedback.

https://packt.link/r/180323248X

Your review is important to us and the tech community and will help us make sure we're delivering excellent quality content.

Section 1 – The Basics of Test-Driven iOS Development

Without a good understanding of the basics, learning is hard and frustrating. In this section, we will learn what unit tests are, how they are connected to test-driven development, and how they look and work in Xcode.

In this section, we will cover the following chapters:

- *Chapter 1, Your First Unit Tests*
- *Chapter 2, Understanding Test-Driven Development*
- *Chapter 3, Test-Driven Development in Xcode*

1
Your First Unit Tests

When the iPhone platform was first introduced, applications were small and focused only on one feature. It was easy to make money with an app that only did one thing (for example, a flashlight app that only showed a white screen). The code of these early apps only had a few hundred lines and could easily be tested by tapping the screen for a few minutes.

Since then, the App Store and the available apps have changed a lot. There are still small apps with a clear focus in the App Store, but it's much harder to make money from them. A common app has many features but still needs to be easy to use. There are companies with several developers working on one app full-time. These apps sometimes have a feature set that is normally found in desktop applications. It is very difficult and time-consuming to test all the features in such apps manually for every update.

One reason for this is that manual testing needs to be done through a **user interface (UI)**, and it takes time to load the app to be tested. In addition to this, human beings are very slow compared to the capabilities of computers for tasks such as testing and verifying computer programs. Most of the time, a computer (or a smartphone) waits for the user's next input. If we could let a computer insert values, testing could be drastically accelerated. In fact, a computer can run several hundred tests within a few seconds. This is exactly what unit tests are all about.

A unit test is a piece of code that executes some other code and checks whether the result is what the developer expected. The word "unit" means that the test executes a small unit of code. Usually, that is one function of a class or some similar type of structure. How big the unit actually is depends on the feature to be tested and on the person who is writing the test.

Writing unit tests seems hard at first because for most developers, it's a new concept. This chapter is aimed at helping you get started with writing your first simple unit tests.

These are the main topics we will cover in the chapter:

- Building your first automatic unit test
- Assert functions in the XCTest framework
- Understanding the difference from other kinds of tests

Technical requirements

All the code in this chapter is uploaded (in complete form) here:

```
https://github.com/PacktPublishing/Test-Driven-iOS-
Development-with-Swift-Fourth-Edition/tree/main/chapter01
```

Building your first automatic unit test

If you have done some iOS development (or application development in general) already, the following example might seem familiar to you.

You are planning to build an app. You start collecting features, drawing some sketches, or your project manager hands the requirements to you. At some point, you start coding. You set up the project and start implementing the required features of the app.

Let's say the app has an input form, and the values the user puts in have to be validated before the data can be sent to the server. The validation checks, for example, whether the email address and the phone number have a valid format. After implementing the form, you want to check whether everything works. But before you can test it manually, you need to write code that presents the form on the screen. Then, you build and run your app in the iOS simulator. The form is somewhere deep in the view hierarchy, so you navigate to the view and put the values into the form. It doesn't work—something is wrong with the phone number validation code. You go back to the code and try to fix the problem. Sometimes, this also means starting the debugger and stepping through the code to find the bug.

Eventually, the validation works for the test data you put in. Normally, you would need to test for all possible values to make sure that the validation not only works for your name and your data, but also for all valid data. But there is this long list of requirements on your desk, and you are already running late. The navigation to the form takes three taps in the simulator and putting in all the different values just takes too long. You are a coder, after all.

If only a robot could perform this testing for you.

What are unit tests?

Automatic unit tests act like this robot for you. They execute code, but without having to navigate to the screen with the feature to test. Instead of running the app over and over again, you write tests with different input data and let the computer test your code in the blink of an eye. Let's see how this works in a simple example.

Implementing a unit test example

In this example, we write a simple function that counts the number of vowels in a string. Proceed as follows:

1. Open Xcode and go to **File | New | Project**.

2. Navigate to **iOS | Application | App** and click on **Next**.

3. Put in the name `FirstDemo`, select `Storyboard` for the **Interface** field and `Swift` for the **Language** field, and check **Include Tests**.

4. Uncheck **Use Core Data** and click on **Next**. The following screenshot shows the options in Xcode:

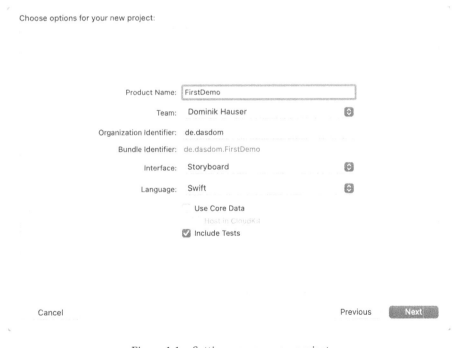

Figure 1.1 – Setting up your new project

Xcode sets up a project ready for development, in addition to two test targets for your unit and your UI tests.

5.   Open the `FirstDemoTests` folder in the project navigator. Within the folder, there is one file: `FirstDemoTests.swift`.

6.   Select `FirstDemoTests.swift` to open it in the editor.

What you see here is a test case. A test case is a class comprising several tests. In the beginning, it's a good practice to have one test case for each class in the main target.

Let's go through this file step by step, as follows:

The file starts with the import of the test framework and the main target, as illustrated here:

```swift
import XCTest
@testable import FirstDemo
```

Every test case needs to import the `XCTest` framework. It defines the `XCTestCase` class and the test assertions that you will see later in this chapter.

The second line imports the `FirstDemo` module. All the code you write for the demo app will be in this module. By default, classes, structs, enums, and their methods are defined with internal access control. This means that they can be accessed only from within the module. But the test code lives outside of the module. To be able to write tests for your code, you need to import the module with the `@testable` keyword. This keyword makes the internal elements of the module accessible in the test case.

Next, we'll take a look at the class declaration, as follows:

```swift
class FirstDemoTests: XCTestCase {
```

Nothing special here. This defines the `FirstDemoTests` class as a subclass of `XCTestCase`.

The first two methods in the class are shown in the following code snippet:

```swift
override func setUpWithError() throws {
  // Put setup code here. This method ...
}


override func tearDownWithError() throws {
  // Put teardown code here. This method ...
}
```

The `setUpWithError()` method is called before the invocation of each test method in the class. Here, you can insert the code that should run before each test. You will see an example of this later in this chapter.

The opposite of `setUpWithError()` is `tearDownWithError()`. This method is called after the invocation of each test method in the class. If you need to clean up after your tests, put the necessary code in this method.

The next two methods are template tests provided by the template authors at Apple:

```swift
func testExample() throws {
    // This is an example of a functional test case.
    // Use XCTAssert and related functions to ...
}

func testPerformanceExample() throws {
    // This is an example of a performance test case.
    self.measure {
        // Put the code you want to measure the time of here.
    }
}
```

The first method is a normal unit test. You will use this kind of test a lot in the course of this book.

The second method is a performance test. It is used to test methods or functions that perform time-critical computations. The code you put into the measure closure is called 10 times, and the average duration is measured. Performance tests can be useful when implementing or improving complex algorithms and to make sure that their performance does not decline. We will not use performance tests in this book.

All the test methods that you write have to have the `test` prefix; otherwise, the test runner can't find and run them. This behavior allows easy disabling of tests—just remove the `test` prefix of the method name. Later, you will take a look at other possibilities to disable some tests without renaming or removing them.

Now, let's implement our first test. Let's assume that you have a method that counts the vowels of a string. A possible implementation looks like this:

```swift
func numberOfVowels(in string: String) -> Int {
    let vowels: [Character] = ["a", "e", "i", "o", "u",
                               "A", "E", "I", "O", "U"]
```

```
    var numberOfVowels = 0
    for character in string {
      if vowels.contains(character) {
        numberOfVowels += 1
      }
    }
    return numberOfVowels
  }
```

I guess this code makes you feel uncomfortable. Please keep calm. Don't throw this book into the corner—we will make this code more "swifty" soon. Add this method to the `ViewController` class in `ViewController.swift`.

This method does the following things:

1. First, an array of characters is defined containing all the vowels in the English alphabet.
2. Next, we define a variable to store the number of vowels. The counting is done by looping over the characters of the string. If the current character is contained in the `vowels` array, `numberOfVowels` is increased by one.
3. Finally, `numberOfVowels` is returned.

Open `FirstDemoTests.swift` and delete the methods with the `test` prefix. Then, add the following method:

```
func test_numberOfVowels_whenGivenDominik_shouldReturn3() {
    let viewController = ViewController()

    let result = viewController.numberOfVowels(in: "Dominik")

    XCTAssertEqual(result, 3,
      "Expected 3 vowels in 'Dominik' but got \(result)")
}
```

This test creates an instance of `ViewController` and assigns it to the `viewController` constant. It calls the function that we want to test and assigns the result to a constant. Finally, the code in the test method calls the `XCTAssertEqual(_:, _:)` function to check whether the result is what we expected. If the two first parameters in `XCTAssertEqual` are equal, the test passes; otherwise, it fails.

To run the tests, select a simulator of your choice and go to **Product | Test**, or use the ⌘*U* shortcut. Xcode compiles the project and runs the test. You will see something similar to this:

```
     ◈      func test_numberOfVowels_whenGivenDominik_shouldReturn3() {
     19          let viewController = ViewController()
     20
     21          let result = viewController.numberOfVowels(in: "Dominik")
     22
     23          XCTAssertEqual(result, 3,
     24                       "Expected 3 vowels in 'Dominik' but got \(result)")
     25      }
```

Figure 1.2 – Xcode shows a green diamond with a checkmark when a test passes

The green diamond with a checkmark on the left-hand side of the editor indicates that the test passed. So, that's it—your first unit test. Step back for a moment and celebrate. This could be the beginning of a new development paradigm for you.

Now that we have a fast test that proves that the numberOfVowels(in:) method does what we intended, we are going to improve the implementation. The method looks like it has been translated from **Objective-C**. But this is Swift. We can do better. Open ViewController.swift, and replace the numberOfVowels(in:) method with this more "swifty" implementation:

```
func numberOfVowels(in string: String) -> Int {
    let vowels: [Character] = ["a", "e", "i", "o", "u",
                               "A", "E", "I", "O", "U"]

    return string.reduce(0) {
        $0 + (vowels.contains($1) ? 1 : 0)
    }
}
```

Here, we make use of the reduce function, which is defined on the array type. The reduce function combines all the elements of a sequence into one value using the provided closure. $0 and $1 are anonymous shorthand arguments representing the current value of the combination and the next item in the sequence. Run the tests again (⌘*U*) to make sure that this implementation works the same as the one earlier.

Disabling slow UI tests

You might have realized that Xcode also runs the UI test in the `FirstDemoUITests` target. UI tests are painfully slow. We don't want to run those tests every time we type the ⌘*U* shortcut. To disable the UI tests, proceed as follows:

1. Open the scheme selection and click on **Edit Scheme…**, as shown in the following screenshot:

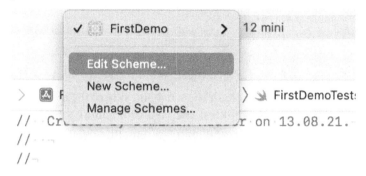

Figure 1.3 – Selecting the target selector to open the scheme editor

2. Xcode opens the scheme editor. Select the **Test** option and uncheck the `FirstDemoUITests` target, as shown in the following screenshot:

Figure 1.4 – Deselecting the UI test target

This disables the UI tests for this scheme, and running tests becomes fast. Check yourself and run the tests using the ⌘U shortcut.

Before we move on, let's recap what we have seen so far. First, you learned that you could easily write code that tests your code. Secondly, you saw that a test helped improve the code because now, you don't have to worry about breaking the feature when changing the implementation.

To check whether the result of the method is as we expected, we used `XCTAssertEqual(_:, _:)`. This is one of many `XCTAssert` functions that are defined in the XCTest framework. The next section shows the most important ones.

Assert functions in the XCTest framework

Each test needs to assert some expected behavior. The use of `XCTAssert` functions tells Xcode what is expected.

A test method without an `XCTAssert` function that doesn't throw an error will always pass.

The most important assert functions are listed here:

- `XCTAssertTrue(_:_:file:line:)`: This asserts that an expression is true.

- `XCTAssert(_:_:file:line:)`: This assertion is the same as `XCTAssertTrue(_:_:file:line:)`.

- `XCTAssertFalse(_:_:file:line:)`: This asserts that an expression is false.

- `XCTAssertEqual(_:_:_:file:line:)`: This asserts that two expressions are equal.

- `XCTAssertEqual(_:_:accuracy:_:file:line:)`: This asserts that two expressions are the same, taking into account the accuracy defined in the `accuracy` parameter.

- `XCTAssertNotEqual(_:_:_:file:line:)`: This asserts that two expressions are not equal.

- `XCTAssertNotEqual(_:_:accuracy:_:file:line:)`: This asserts that two expressions are not the same, taking into account the accuracy defined in the `accuracy` parameter.

- `XCTAssertNil(_:_:file:line:)`: This asserts that an expression is nil.

- `XCTAssertNotNil(_:_:file:line:)`: This asserts that an expression is not nil.

- `XCTFail(_:file:line:)`: This always fails.

To take a look at a full list of the available `XCTAssert` functions, press *Ctrl* and click on the `XCTAssertEqual` word in the test that you have just written. Then, select **Jump to Definition** in the pop-up menu, as shown in the following screenshot:

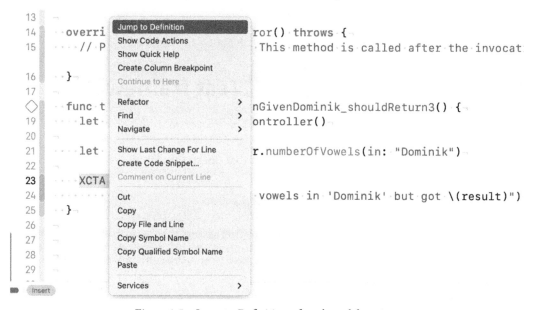

Figure 1.5 – Jump to Definition of a selected function

Note that most `XCTAssert` functions can be replaced with `XCTAssert(_:_:file:line)`. For example, the following assert functions are asserting the same thing:

```
// This assertion asserts the same as...
XCTAssertEqual(2, 1+1, "2 should be the same as 1+1")


// ...this assertion
XCTAssertTrue(2 == 1+1, "2 should be the same as 1+1")
```

But you should use more precise assertions whenever possible, as the log output of the more precise assertion methods tells you exactly what happened in case of a failure. For example, look at the log output of the following two assertions:

```
XCTAssertEqual(1, 2)
// Log output:
// XCTAssertEqual failed: ("1") is not equal to ("2")
```

```
XCTAssert(1 == 2)
// Log output:
// XCTAssertTrue failed
```

In the first case, you don't need to look at the test to understand what happened. The log tells you exactly what went wrong.

Custom assert functions

But sometimes, even the more precise assert function is not precise enough. In this case, you can write your own assert functions. As an example, let's assume we have a test that asserts that two dictionaries have the same content. If we used XCTAssertEqual to test that, the log output would look like this:

```
func test_dictsAreQual() {
  let dict1 = ["id": "2", "name": "foo"]
  let dict2 = ["id": "2", "name": "fo"]

  XCTAssertEqual(dict1, dict2)
  // Log output:
  // XCTAssertEqual failed: ("["name": "foo", "id":
    "2"]")...
  // ...is not equal to ("["name": "fo", "id": "2"]")
}
```

For the short dictionaries in this example, finding the difference is quite easy. But what if the dictionary has 20 entries or even more? When we add the following assert function to the test target, we get better log outputs:

```
func DDHAssertEqual<A: Equatable, B: Equatable>
  (_ first: [A:B],
   _ second: [A:B]) {

  if first == second {
    return
  }

  for key in first.keys {
    if first[key] != second[key] {
      let value1 = String(describing: first[key]!)
      let value2 = String(describing: second[key]!)
      let keyValue1 = "\"\(key)\": \(value1)"
      let keyValue2 = "\"\(key)\": \(value2)"
      let message = "\(keyValue1) is not equal to
        \(keyValue2)"
      XCTFail(message)
      return
    }
  }
}
```

This method compares the values for each key and fails if one of the values differs. Additionally, this assert function should check whether the dictionaries have the same keys. This functionality is left as an exercise for the reader. Here, we focus this example on how to write a custom assert function. By keeping the example short, the main point is easier to understand.

When we run this test with the preceding dictionaries, we see the following output in Xcode:

```
❖     func test_comparingDictionariesWithCustomAssertFunction() {
28       let dict1 = ["id": "2", "name": "foo"]
29       let dict2 = ["id": "2", "name": "fo"]
30
31       DDHAssertEqual(dict1, dict2)        ❖  failed - "name": foo is not equal to "name": fo
32     }
33   }
34
35   func DDHAssertEqual<A: Equatable, B: Equatable>(_ first: [A:B],
36                                                   _ second: [A:B]) {
37
38     if first == second {
39       return
40     }
41
42     for key in first.keys {
43
44       if first[key] != second[key] {
45         let value1 = String(describing: first[key]!)
46         let value2 = String(describing: second[key]!)
47         let keyValue1 = "\"\(key)\": \(value1)"
48         let keyValue2 = "\"\(key)\": \(value2)"
49         let message = "\(keyValue1) is not equal to \(keyValue2)"
50         XCTFail(message)             ❖  failed - "name": foo is not equal to "name": fo
51         return
52       }
53     }
54   }
```

Figure 1.6 – Xcode showing the failure at two different places

As you can see in the preceding screenshot, Xcode shows the test failure in the assert function. In the test method, it only shows a redirect to the failure. Fortunately, there is an easy fix for that. All we have to do is to pass file and line parameters to the custom assert function and use these in the XCTFail call, like this:

```
func DDHAssertEqual<A: Equatable, B: Equatable>(
  _ first: [A:B],
  _ second: [A:B],
  file: StaticString = #filePath,      // << new
  line: UInt = #line) {                // << new

  if first == second {
    return
  }
```

```
        for key in first.keys {

        if first[key] != second[key] {
            let value1 = String(describing: first[key]!)
            let value2 = String(describing: second[key]!)
            let keyValue1 = "\"\(key)\": \(value1)"
            let keyValue2 = "\"\(key)\": \(value2)"
            let message = "\(keyValue1) is not equal to
               \(keyValue2)"
            XCTFail(message, file: file, line: line)   // << new
            return
            }
        }
    }
```

Note that our assert function now has two new parameters: file and line, with the default values #filePath and #line, respectively. When the function is called in a test method, these default parameters make sure that the file path and the line of the call site are passed into that assert function. These parameters are then forwarded into the XCTAssert functions (XCTFail in our case, but this works with all XCT... functions). As a result, the failure is now shown in the line in which the DDHAssertEqual function is called, and we didn't have to change the call of the assert function. The following screenshot illustrates this:

```
26
◆    func test_comparingDictionariesWithCustomAssertFunction() {
28        let dict1 = ["id": "2", "name": "foo"]
29        let dict2 = ["id": "2", "name": "fo"]
30
31        DDHAssertEqual(dict1, dict2)      ◇ failed - "name": foo is not equal to "name": fo
32    }
33  }
```

Figure 1.7 – Improved failure reporting

This example shows how easy it is to write your own assert functions that behave like the ones that come with Xcode. Custom assert functions can improve the readability of the test code, but keep in mind that this is also code you have to maintain.

Understanding the difference from other kinds of tests

Unit tests are just one piece of a good test suite. In my opinion, they are the most important tests because when carried out correctly, they are fast, focused, and easy to understand. But to increase your confidence in your code, you should additionally add integration, UI/snapshot, and manual tests. What are those?

Integration tests

In integration tests, the feature that is being tested is not isolated from the rest of the code. With these kinds of tests, the developer tries to figure out if the different units (that are thoroughly tested with unit tests) interact with each other as required. As a result, integration tests execute real database queries and fetch data from live servers, which makes them significantly slower than unit tests. They are not run as often as unit tests and failures are more difficult to understand as the error has to be tracked down in all involved code units.

UI tests

As the name suggests, UI tests run on the UI of an app. A computer program (the test runner) executes the app as a user would do. Usually, this means that in such a test assertion, we also have to use information accessible on screen. This means a UI test can only test whether a feature works as required when the result is visible on screen. In addition, these tests are usually quite slow as the test runner often has to wait until animations and screen updates are finished.

Snapshot tests

Snapshot tests compare the UI with previously taken snapshots. If a defined percentage of pixels differs from the snapshot image, the test fails. This makes them a perfect fit for situations where the UI of one app screen is already finished and you want to make sure that it won't change for given test data.

Manual tests

The final kind of test in the development of an app is a manual test. Even if you have hundreds of unit and integration tests, real people using your app will most probably find a bug. To minimize the number of bugs your users can find, you need testers in your team or to ask some users for feedback on the beta version of your app. The more diverse the group of beta testers is, the more bugs they will find before your app ships.

In this book, we will only cover unit tests because **test-driven development (TDD)** only works reasonably well with fast reliable feedback.

Summary

In this chapter, we discussed what unit tests are and saw some easy unit tests in action. We learned about the different assert functions available in XCTest, the testing framework provided by Apple. By writing our own assert function, we learned to improve the log output and what needs to be done to make it behave like built-in functions. This chapter concluded with other kinds of tests and how they differ from unit tests.

In the next chapter, we will learn what TDD is, and what its advantages and disadvantages are.

Exercises

1. Write an assert function that only fails when the keys in two dictionaries differ. This assert function should also fail if a key is missing in one of the dictionaries.

2. Improve DDHAssertEqual<A: Equatable, B: Equatable>(_:_:file:line:) such that it also checks the keys of the dictionaries.

2
Understanding Test-Driven Development

Now that we have seen what unit tests are and how they can help in development, we are going to learn about **test-driven development** (**TDD**).

After giving you some insights into the origin and objective of TDD, we will move ahead and have a look at the benefits and drawbacks of it. By the end of the chapter, you will have a clear idea about the relevance of TDD and what should be or can be tested using it.

These are the main topics that we will cover in the chapter:

- The origin of TDD
- The TDD workflow
- Advantages of TDD
- Disadvantages of TDD
- What to test

The origin of TDD

In 1996, Kent Beck, Ward Cunningham, and Ron Jeffries introduced a new software development methodology called **Extreme Programming** while they were working on the project *Comprehensive Compensation System* at Chrysler. The word *Extreme* indicates that the concepts behind Extreme Programming are totally different from the concepts used in software development back then. For many people, these concepts sound extreme even today.

The methodology is based on 12 rules or practices. One of the rules states that developers have to write unit tests and all parts of the software have to be thoroughly tested. All tests have to pass before the software (or a new feature) can be released to customers. The tests should be written before the production code that they test.

This so-called test-first programming led to TDD. As the name suggests, in TDD, tests drive the development. This means that the developer writes code only because there is a test that fails. The tests dictate whether the code has to be written, and they also provide a measure when a feature is "done" – it is done when all tests for the feature pass.

This might sound silly to you if you haven't done any TDD before. You have to try and keep with it for some time to see the advantages and that it's not silly but rather quite clever. In TDD you always focus on one feature of the product you are building. And as you have tests for all the features you have built before, you don't have to keep the details of the rest of the code in mind. You can trust in the existing tests and that you won't break something that worked before.

Because of the focus on just one feature at a time, you will have a working piece of software almost all the time. So, when your boss enters your office and asks you for a demonstration of the current status of the project, you are only a few minutes away from a presentable (that is, compiled) and thoroughly tested piece of software.

Now that we know what TDD refers to, let's look into its workflow.

The TDD workflow – red, green, refactor

The normal workflow of TDD comprises three steps – *red, green, refactor*. The following sections describe these steps in detail.

Red

You start by writing a failing test. It needs to test a required feature of the software product that is not already implemented or an edge case that you want to make sure is covered. The name red comes from the way most IDEs indicate a failing test. Xcode uses a red diamond with a white x on it as shown in the following figure:

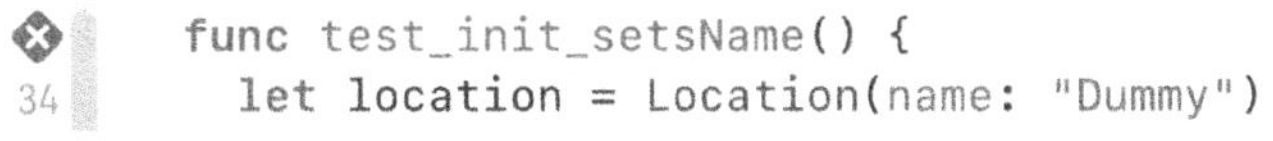

```
func test_init_setsName() {
    let location = Location(name: "Dummy")
```

Figure 2.1 – Xcode marks a failing test with a white cross in a red diamond

It is very important that the test you write in this step initially fails. Otherwise, you can't ensure that the test works and really tests the feature that you want to implement. It could be that you have written a test that always passes and is, therefore, useless. Or, it is possible that the feature is already implemented. Either way, you gain insight into your code.

Green

In the green step, you write the simplest code that makes the test pass. It doesn't matter whether the code you write is good and clean. The code can also be silly and even wrong. It is enough when all the tests pass. The name green refers to how most IDEs indicate a passing test. Xcode uses a green diamond with a white checkmark.

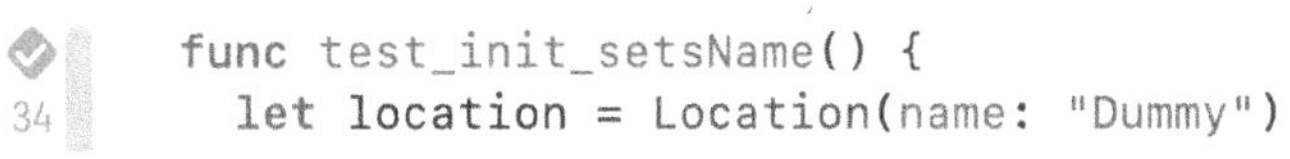

```
func test_init_setsName() {
    let location = Location(name: "Dummy")
```

Figure 2.2 – Xcode marks a passing test with a white checkmark in a green diamond

It is very important that you try to write the simplest code that makes the test pass. By doing so, you only write code that you actually need and that is the simplest implementation possible. When I say simple, I mean that it should be easy to read, understand, and change. Test code should always be easy to understand. Try to write your tests such that you understand them even when you haven't worked on them for months. When tests break, it's often while you are working on something completely different. A clear and easy-to-understand test helps you to find the problem quickly and get back to the context you were working on.

Often the simplest implementation will not be enough for the feature you're trying to implement, but still enough to make all the tests pass. This just means that you need another failing test to further drive the development of that feature.

Refactor

During the green step, you write just enough code to make all the tests pass again. As I just mentioned, it doesn't matter what the code looks like in the green step. In the refactor step you improve the code. You remove duplication, extract common values, and so on. Do what is needed to make the code as good as possible. The tests help you to not break already implemented features while refactoring.

> **Important Note**
> Don't skip this step. Always try to think about how you can improve the code after you have implemented a feature. Doing so helps to keep the code clean and maintainable. This ensures that it is always in good shape.

As you have written only a few lines of code since the last refactor step, the changes needed to make the code clean shouldn't take much time.

The advantages of TDD

TDD comes with advantages and disadvantages. These are the main advantages:

- **You only write code that is needed**: You should stop writing production code when all your tests pass and you can't think of another test to write. If your project needs another feature, you need a test to drive the implementation of that feature. The code you write is the simplest code possible. So, all the code ending up in the product is actually needed to implement the features.

- **More modular design**: In TDD, you concentrate on one microfeature at a time. And as you write the test first, the code automatically becomes easy to test. Code that is easy to test has a clear interface. This results in a modular design for your app.

- **Easier to maintain**: As the different parts of your app are decoupled from each other and have clear interfaces, the code becomes easier to maintain. You can exchange the implementation of a microfeature with a better implementation without affecting another module. You could even keep the tests and rewrite the complete app. When all the tests pass, you are done.

- **Easier to refactor**: Every feature is thoroughly tested. You don't need to be afraid to make drastic changes because if all the tests still pass, everything is fine. This point is very important because you, as a developer, improve your skills each and every day. If you open the project after 6 months of working on something else, most probably, you'll have many ideas on how to improve the code. But your memory about all the different parts and how they fit together won't be fresh anymore. So, making changes can be dangerous. With a complete test suite, you can easily improve the code without the fear of breaking your app.

- **High test coverage**: There is a test for every feature. This results in high test coverage. High test coverage helps you gain confidence in your code.

- **Tests document the code**: Test code shows how your code is meant to be used. As such, it documents your code. Test code is sample code that shows what the code does and how the interface has to be used.

- **Less debugging**: How often have you wasted a day finding a nasty bug? How often have you copied an error message from Xcode and searched for it on the internet? With TDD, you write fewer bugs because the tests tell you early on whether you've made a mistake. And the bugs you write are found much earlier. You can concentrate on fixing bugs when your memory is still fresh about what the code is supposed to do and how it does it.

In the next section, we'll discuss the disadvantages of TDD.

The disadvantages of TDD

Just like everything else in the world, TDD has some disadvantages. The main ones are listed here:

- **No silver bullet**: Tests help to find bugs, but they can't find all bugs that you introduce in the test code and implementation code. If you haven't understood the problem you need to solve, writing tests most probably won't help.

- **It seems slower at the beginning**: When you start TDD, you will get the feeling that it takes longer to make easy implementations. You need to think about the interfaces, write the test code, and run the tests before you can finally start writing the code.

- **All the members of a team need to do it**: As TDD influences the design of code, it is recommended that either all the members of a team use TDD or no one at all. In addition to this, it's sometimes difficult to justify TDD to management because they often have the feeling that the implementation of new features takes longer if developers write code that won't end up in the product half of the time. It helps if the whole team agrees on the importance of unit tests.

- **Tests need to be maintained when requirements change**: Probably, the strongest argument against TDD is that the tests have to be maintained just as the code has to. Whenever requirements change, you need to change the code and tests. But you are working with TDD. This means that you need to change the tests first, and then make the tests pass. So, in reality, tests help you to understand the new requirements and implement the code without breaking other features.

Beginners often ask which part of their code they should write tests for. The following section tries to find an answer to that.

What to test

What should be tested? When using TDD and following its ideology, the answer is easy – everything. You only write production code because there is a failing test.

In practice, it's not that easy. For example, should the position and color of a button be tested? Should the view hierarchy be tested? Probably not; the color and exact position of the button is not important for the functioning of an app. In the early stages of development, these kinds of things tend to change. With Auto Layout, different screen sizes, and different localizations of apps, the exact position of buttons and labels depends on many parameters.

In general, you should test the features that make the app useful for a user and those that need to work. Users don't care whether the button is exactly 20 points from the rightmost edge of the screen. Users seek apps that are easy to understand and a joy to use.

In addition to this, you should not test the whole app at once using unit tests. Unit tests are meant to test small units of computation. They need to be fast and reliable. Things such as database access and networking should be tested using integration tests, where the tests drive the real finished app. Integration tests are allowed to be slow because they are run a lot less often than unit tests. Usually, they are run with the help of a continuous integration system each night on a server, where it doesn't matter that the complete test suite takes several minutes (or even hours) to execute.

Summary

In this chapter, we dipped our toes into the new waters of TDD in general. The chapter showed the workflow of TDD – red, green, refactor – which we will use throughout this book to build an app. In addition, we have seen what the advantages and the disadvantages of TDD are.

In the following chapter, we will explore how TDD works in Xcode, the tool most of us use to build iOS apps.

3
Test-Driven Development in Xcode

For **test-driven development** (**TDD**), we need a way to write and execute unit tests. We could write the tests into the main target of our Xcode project but that would be impractical. We would have to separate the test code from the production code somehow, and we would have to write some scripts that execute the text code and gather feedback about the results of the tests.

Fortunately, this has already been done. It all started in 1998, when the Swiss company Sen:te developed OCUnit, a testing framework for Objective-C (hence the OC prefix). OCUnit was a port of SUnit, a testing framework that Kent Beck had written for Smalltalk in 1994.

With Xcode 2.1, Apple added OCUnit to Xcode. One reason for this step was that they used it to develop Core Data at the same time that they developed Tiger, the OS with which Core Data was shipped. Bill Bumgarner, an Apple engineer, wrote this later in a blog post:

> *"Core Data 1.0 is not perfect, but it is a rock solid product that I'm damned proud of. The quality and performance achieved could not have been done without the use of unit testing. Furthermore, we were able to perform highly disruptive operations to the codebase very late in the development cycle. The end result was a vast increase in performance, a much cleaner codebase, and rock solid release."*

Apple realized how valuable unit tests can be when developing complex systems in a changing environment. They wanted third-party developers to benefit from unit tests as well. OCUnit could be (and has been) added to Xcode by hand before version 2.1. But by including it in the **Integrated Development Environment** (**IDE**), the investment in time that was needed to start unit testing was reduced a lot, and as a result, more people started to write tests.

In 2008, OCUnit was integrated into the iPhone SDK 2.2 to allow unit testing of iPhone apps.

Finally, in 2013, unit testing became a first-class citizen in Xcode 5 with the introduction of XCTest. With XCTest, Apple added specific user interface elements to Xcode that helped with testing, which allowed running specific tests, finding failing tests quickly, and getting an overview of all the tests. We will go over the testing user interface in Xcode later in this chapter. But, first, we will take a look at TDD using Xcode in action. This chapter sets the foundation we need to start building our first app using TDD.

These are the main sections we will cover in this chapter:

- An example of TDD
- Finding information about tests in Xcode
- Running tests
- Setting up and tearing down
- Debugging tests

Technical requirements

All the code in this chapter is uploaded (in complete form) here:

```
https://github.com/PacktPublishing/Test-Driven-iOS-
Development-with-Swift-Fourth-Edition/tree/main/chapter03
```

An example of TDD

For this TDD example, we are going to use the same project we created in *Chapter 1, Your First Unit Tests*. Open the FirstDemo project in Xcode, and run the tests by hitting ⌘U. The test we wrote to explore the custom assert function is failing. We don't need this test anymore. Delete it.

Let's say we are building an app for a blogging platform. When writing a new post, the user puts in a headline for the post. All the words in the headline should start with an uppercase letter.

To start the TDD workflow, we need a failing test. The following questions need to be considered when writing the test:

- **Precondition**: What is the state of the system before we invoke the method?
- **Invocation**: How should the signature of the method look? What are the input parameters (if any) of the method?
- **Assertion**: What is the expected result of the method invocation?

For our blogging app example, here are some possible answers to these questions:

- **Precondition**: None.
- **Invocation**: The method should take a string and it should return a string. A possible name for that method is makeHeadline.
- **Assertion**: The resulting string should be the same, but all the words should start with an uppercase letter.

This is enough to get us started. Enter the red step.

Capitalize headline – red

The following steps bring us to the first red state of our TDD journey:

1. Open `FirstDemoTests.swift`, and add the following code to the `FirstDemoTests` class:

    ```
    // FirstDemoTests.swift
    func
     test_makeHeadline_shouldCapitalisePassedInString() {
      let blogger = Blogger()
    }
    ```

    This isn't a complete test method yet because we aren't really testing anything. But we have to stop writing the test at this point because the compiler complains that it **Cannot find 'Blogger' in scope**. The test assumes that there is a class or a struct called `Blogger` but we haven't added it yet.

    Following the TDD workflow, we need to add code until the compiler stops printing errors. Remember that **code does not compile** within a test means "the test is failing." And a failing test means we need to write code until the test does not fail anymore.

2. Add a Swift file `Blogger.swift` to the main target with the following code:

    ```
    // Blogger.swift
    import Foundation
    struct Blogger {
    }
    ```

    Xcode replaces the error in the test with a warning that we do not use the `blogger` variable. That's true. So let's use it.

3. Change the test code such that it looks like this:

    ```
    // FirstDemoTests.swift
    func
     test_makeHeadline_shouldCapitalisePassedInString() {
      let blogger = Blogger()

      let headline = blogger.makeHeadline(from: "the
        Accessibility inspector")
    }
    ```

The test is still not complete. But again we have to stop because the compiler is complaining, this time with the message **Value of type 'Blogger' has no member 'makeHeadline'**. So even with these few lines of code, you can already see how the test is "driving" the development. Step by step, we add code to the test and to the production code to implement the feature we are trying to build.

4. As the test is failing (not compiling) right now, we need to switch back to the `Blogger` struct and add some more code:

```
// Blogger.swift

struct Blogger {
    func makeHeadline(from input: String) -> String {
        return ""
    }
}
```

Again, this changes the error in the test code to a warning that we are not using the headline variable. This is true. But we aren't finished with the test yet.

5. We will use the variable next. Add the following assertion to the test method:

```
// FirstDemoTests.swift

func
  test_makeHeadline_shouldCapitalisePassedInString() {
    let blogger = Blogger()

    let headline = blogger.makeHeadline(from: "the
      Accessibility inspector")

    XCTAssertEqual(headline, "The Accessibility
      Inspector")
}
```

This makes the test compile. Run the tests with the keyboard shortcut ⌘ U.

The test we just added compiles and fails. We can move on to the green phases in the TDD workflow.

Capitalize headline – green

The test fails because the string that is returned from `makeHeadline(from:)` is just an empty string. But the method should return the capitalized version of the input string `The Accessibility inspector`.

Following the TDD workflow, we need to go back to the implementation and add the simplest code that makes the test pass. In `Blogger.swift`, change the code of `makeHeadline(from:)` such that it reads like this:

```swift
func makeHeadline(from input: String) -> String {
    return "The Accessibility Inspector"
}
```

This code is stupid and wrong, but it is the simplest code that makes the test pass. Run the tests (⌘ U) to make sure that this is actually the case.

Even though the code we just wrote is useless for the feature we are trying to implement, it still has value for us, the developers. It tells us that we need another test.

Capitalize headline – refactor

Before writing more tests, we need to refactor the existing ones. In the production code, there is nothing to refactor. This code couldn't be simpler or more elegant.

But the test can be improved. Right now, the relevant information for the test is kind of unstructured. It's not a big problem but maybe we can improve the readability of the test by following these steps:

1. Replace the `test_makeHeadline_shouldCapitalisePassedInString()` test method with the following code:

```swift
func
  test_makeHeadline_shouldCapitalisePassedInString() {
    let blogger = Blogger()
    let input = "the Accessibility inspector"

    let result = blogger.makeHeadline(from: input)

    let expected = "The Accessibility Inspector"
    XCTAssertEqual(result, expected)
}
```

By using variables in the test, we make it easier to understand. The names of the variables inform the reader of the test about the purpose of these values. One value is the input, one is the result, and one is the expected value.

Run the tests. All the tests should still pass. But how do we know whether the tests still test the same thing as they did earlier? In most cases, the changes we'll make while refactoring the tests don't need to be tested themselves. But, sometimes (such as in this case), it is good to make sure that the test still works. This means that we need a failing test again.

2. Go to makeHeadline(from:) and change the returned string like this:

```
func makeHeadline(from input: String) -> String {
    return "The Accessibility"
}
```

We have removed the last word from the return string. Run the tests again to make sure that the test now fails.

3. Now change the returned string back to The Accessibility Inspector to make the test pass again. Confirm that all tests pass again by running the tests.

By making the test fail on purpose and fixing it in the next step, we have proven that the test can fail. This is important because writing a test that always passes can easily happen. For example, if you forget to add an assert function or the assert function is never reached because of some conditionals in the test, the test is always reported as green.

Note
Always confirm that the test can fail!

We already know that the implementation is not correct. The makeHeadline(from:) method always returns the same string and ignores the string that gets passed into the method. But all tests we have passed. When all tests pass, but we know that we are not finished with the feature yet, this means we need another test. In TDD, we always start with a failing test.

Capitalize headline 2 – red

The production code we have written to make the previous test pass only works for one specific headline. But the feature we want to implement has to work for all possible headlines. Add the following test to `FirstDemoTests.swift`:

```
// FirstDemoTests.swift
func test_makeHeadline_shouldCapitalisePassedInString_2() {
  let blogger = Blogger()
  let input = "The contextual action menu"

  let result = blogger.makeHeadline(from: input)

  let expected = "The Contextual Action Menu"
  XCTAssertEqual(result, expected)
}
```

Run the tests. This new test obviously fails. Now, take a break. Go for a walk or prepare some beverages. Seriously, go away from the computer for half an hour or so.

Let's make the tests green.

Capitalize headline 2 – green

Open `Blogger.swift`, and replace the implementation of `makeHeadline(from:)` with the following code:

```
// Blogger.swift
func makeHeadline(from input: String) -> String {
  let words = input.components(separatedBy: " ")
  var headline = ""
  for var word in words {
    let firstCharacter = word.remove(at: word.startIndex)
    headline +=
      "\(String(firstCharacter).uppercased())\(word) "
  }
  headline.remove(at: headline.index(before:
    headline.endIndex))
  return headline
}
```

It's OK to be shocked by this implementation. With this code, I'm trying to make the point that, in the green step of TDD, any code is good as long as it makes the test pass. We'll improve this code in the next section.

Let's go through this implementation step by step:

1. Split the string into words.

2. Iterate over the words, and remove the first character and change it to uppercase. Add the changed character to the beginning of the word. Add this word with a trailing space to the headline string.

3. Remove the last space and return the string.

Run the tests. All the tests pass. The next thing to perform in the TDD workflow is refactoring.

> **Tip**
>
> Do not skip refactoring. This step is as important as the red and the green step. You are not done until there is nothing to refactor anymore.

Capitalize headline 2 – refactor

Let's start our refactoring with the tests:

1. The two `makeHeadline` tests both start with creating an instance of `Blogger`. This is a repetition of code and a good candidate for refactoring.

    Add the following property at the beginning of the `FirstDemoTests` class:

    ```swift
    // FirstDemoTests.swift
    var blogger: Blogger!
    ```

2. Remember that the `setUp()` method is called before each test is executed. So, it is the perfect place to initialize the `blogger` property:

    ```swift
    // FirstDemoTests.swift
    override func setUpWithError() throws {
        blogger = Blogger()
    }
    ```

3. Each test should clean up after it has run. So, add the following code to
    tearDownWithError():

```
// FirstDemoTests.swift
override func tearDownWithError() throws {
    blogger = nil
}
```

4. Now we can remove the let blogger = Blogger() line from the headline
    tests. Run the tests to make sure that they still compile and run.

5. Now we need to refactor the implementation code. The implementation we have
    right now looks like it was translated from Objective-C to Swift (if you haven't
    used Objective-C yet, you have to trust me on this). But Swift is different and has
    many concepts that make it possible to write less code that is easier to read. Let's
    make the implementation swifter. Replace makeHeadline(from:) with the
    following code:

```
// Blogger.swift
func makeHeadline(from input: String) -> String {
    return input.capitalized
}
```

How cool is that? Swift even comes with a method on the String class to do exactly that.
Run the tests again to make sure we didn't break anything with the refactoring. All the
tests should still pass.

A recap

In this section, we have added a feature to our project using the TDD workflow. We
started with a failing test. We made the test pass. And, finally, we refactored the code to be
clean. The steps you have seen here seem so simple and insignificant that you may think
that you could skip some of the tests and still be good. But then it's not TDD anymore.
The beauty of TDD is that the steps are so easy that you do not have to think about them.
You just have to remember what the next step is.

Because the steps and the rules are so easy, you don't have to waste your brainpower
thinking about what the steps actually mean. The only thing you have to remember is
red, green, and refactor. As a result, you can concentrate on the difficult part: *writing tests,*
making them pass, and *improving code.*

Now that we know how to write tests, let's see where we can find information about our
tests in Xcode.

Finding information about tests in Xcode

With Xcode 5 and the introduction of XCTest, unit testing became tightly integrated into Xcode. Apple added many UI elements to navigate to tests, run specific tests, and find information about failing tests. Over the years, they improved the integration further. One key element here is the **test navigator**.

Test navigator

To open the test navigator, click the diamond with the minus sign in the navigator panel or use the shortcut ⌘ 6:

Figure 3.1 – The test navigator in Xcode

The test navigator shows all tests in the open project or workspace. In the preceding screenshot, you can see the test navigator for our demo project. In the project, there are two test targets, one for the unit tests and one for the UI tests. For complex apps, it can be useful to have more than one unit tests target, but this is beyond the scope of this book. The number of tests is shown right behind the name of the test target. In our case, there are three tests in the unit tests target.

At the bottom of the navigator is a filter control with which you can filter the shown tests. As soon as you start typing, the shown tests are filtered using fuzzy matching. There's a button in the control showing a diamond with a cross:

Figure 3.2 – The button in the test navigator to only show the failing tests

If this button is selected, only the failing tests are shown in the list. With the button on the right, you can filter all skipped tests.

Test overview

Xcode also has a test overview where all the results of the tests are collected in one place. To open it, select **Report navigator** in the navigator panel, and select the last test in the list:

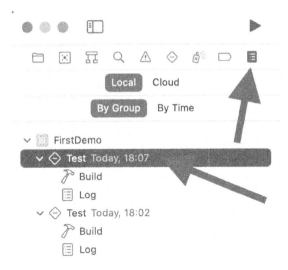

Figure 3.3 – Access the overview of the tests in the report navigator

You can also select other tests in the list if you want to compare test runs with each other. In the editor on the right-hand side, an overview of all the tests from the selected test run is shown:

Figure 3.4 – Overview of the tests of the last test run

When you hover over one of the tests with the mouse pointer, a circle with an arrow to the right appears. If you click on the arrow, Xcode opens the test in the editor.

In the report navigator, there is also the **Log** item. It shows all the tests in a tree-like structure. Here is an example of what this looks like:

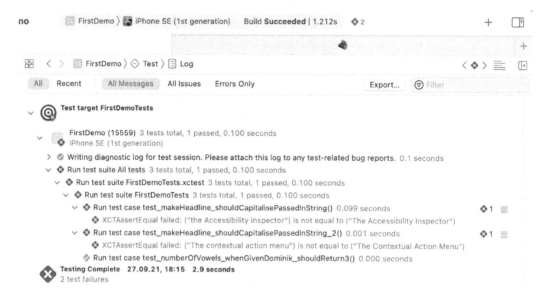

Figure 3.5 – Log of the test reports

The logs show the test cases (in this example, one test case) and the tests within the test cases (in this example, two failing and one passing test). In addition to this, you can also seethe time each test case and even each test needs to execute.

In TDD, it is important for the tests to execute quickly. You want to be able to execute the whole test suite in less than a second. Otherwise, the whole workflow is dominated by test execution and testing can distract your focus and concentration. You should never be tempted to switch to another application (such as Safari) because the tests will take half a minute.

If you notice that the test suite takes too long to be practical, open the logs and search for the tests that slow down testing and try to make the tests faster.

Now that we have seen where we can find information about our tests, in the next section we will explore the different ways to run tests.

Running tests

Xcode provides many different ways to execute tests. You have already seen two ways to execute all the tests in the test suite: go to the **Project | Test** menu item or use the ⌘U keyboard shortcut.

Running one specific test

In TDD, you normally want to run all the tests as often as possible. Running the tests gives you confidence that the code does what you intended when you wrote the tests. In addition to this, you want immediate feedback (that is, a failing test) whenever new code breaks a seemingly unrelated feature. Immediate feedback means that your memory of the changes that broke the feature is fresh, and the fix is made quickly.

Nevertheless, sometimes, you need to run one specific test, but don't let it become a habit. To run one specific test, you can click on the diamond visible next to the test method:

```swift
func test_makeHeadline_shouldCapitalisePassedInString_2() {
    let input = "The contextual action menu"

    let result = blogger.makeHeadline(from: input)

    let expected = "The Contextual Action Menu"
    XCTAssertEqual(result, expected)
}
```

Figure 3.6 – Run one specific test by clicking the diamond next to the test method in the gutter

When you click on it, the production code is compiled and launched in the simulator or on the device, and the test is executed.

There is another way to execute exactly one specific test. When you open the test navigator and hover over one test, a circle with a play icon is shown next to the test method name:

Figure 3.7 – Click the diamond next to the test in the test navigator to run this test

Again, if you click on this test, it is run exclusively.

The test framework identifies tests by the prefix of the method name. If you want to run all tests but one, remove the `test` prefix from the beginning of this test's method name.

Running all tests in a test case

In the same way as running one specific test, you can run all the tests of a specific test case. Click on the diamond next to the definition of the test case, or click on the play button that appears when you hover over the test case name in the test navigator.

Running a group of tests

You can choose to run a group of tests by editing the build scheme. To edit the build scheme, click on the scheme in the toolbar in Xcode, and then click on **Edit Scheme...**:

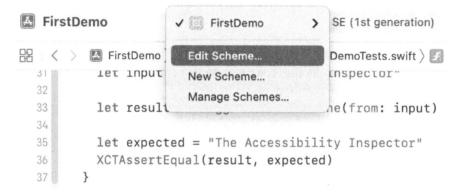

Figure 3.8 – Open the scheme editor

Then, select **Test**, and expand the test suite by clicking on the small triangle. On the right-hand side, there is a column called **Tests**:

Figure 3.9 – Test setting in the scheme editor

The selected scheme only runs the tests that are checked. By default, all the tests are checked, but you can uncheck some tests if you need to. But don't forget to check all the tests again when you are finished.

As an alternative, you can add a build scheme for a group of tests that you want to run regularly without running all tests.

But as mentioned earlier, you should run the complete test suite as often as possible.

The following section shows how to add code that is run before and after each test invocation.

Setting up and tearing down

We have already seen the setUpWithError() and tearDownWithError() instance methods earlier in this chapter. The code in the setUpWithError() instance method is run before each test invocation. In our example, we used setUpWithError() to initialize the Blogger that we wanted to test. As it was run before each test invocation, each test used its own instance of Blogger. The changes we made to this particular instance in one test didn't affect the other test. The tests are executed independently of each other.

The `tearDownWithError()` instance method is run after each test invocation. Use `tearDownWithError()` to perform the necessary cleanup. In the example, we set the `blogger` to `nil` in the `tearDownWithError()` method.

In addition to the instance methods, there are also the `setUp()` and `tearDown()` class methods. These are run before and after all the tests of a test case, respectively.

Debugging tests

Sometimes, but not often, you may need to debug your tests. As with normal code, you can set breakpoints in test code. The debugger then stops the execution of the code at that breakpoint. You can also set breakpoints in the code that will be tested to check whether you have missed something or whether the code you'd like to test is actually executed.

To get a feeling of how this works, let's add an error to a test in the preceding example and debug it:

1. Open `FirstDemoTests.swift` and replace the test method `test_makeHeadline_shouldCapitalisePassedInString_2()` with this code:

    ```
    // FirstDemoTests.swift
    func
      test_makeHeadline_shouldCapitalisePassedInString_2()
      {
        let input = "The contextual action menu"

        let result = blogger.makeHeadline(from: input)

        let expected = "The ContextuaI Action Menu"
        XCTAssertEqual(result, expected)
      }
    ```

    Have you seen the error that we have introduced? The value of the string expected has a typo. The last character in `Contextual` is an uppercase "i" and not a lowercase "l". Run the tests. The test fails and Xcode tells you what the problem is.

2. But for the sake of this exercise, let's set a breakpoint in the line with the `XCTAssertEqual()` function. Click on the area on the left-hand side of the line where you want to set a breakpoint. You have to click on the area next to the red diamond. As a result, your editor will look similar to the following:

```
    ◆      func test_makeHeadline_shouldCapitalisePassedInString_2() {
   40          let input = "The contextual action menu"
   41
   42          let result = blogger.makeHeadline(from: input)
   43
   44          let expected = "The ContextuaI Action Menu"
   45          XCTAssertEqual(result, expected)  ◆  XCTAssertEqual failed: ("The Contextual Act...
   46      }
```

Figure 3.10 – Add a breakpoint in the line with the assertion

3. Run the tests again. The execution of the tests stops at the breakpoint. Open the debug console if it is not already open (go to **View | Debug Area | Activate Console**). In the console, some test output is visible. The last line starts with (lldb) and a blinking cursor. Put in po expected and hit *Return*. po is the "print object" command. As the name suggests, it prints a representation of the object:

```
(lldb) po expected
"The ContextuaI Action Menu"
```

4. Now print the value of the result:

```
(lldb) po result
"The Contextual Action Menu"
```

So, with the help of the debugger, you can find out what is happening.

As we have seen, the debugger is attached to the running app when we run the tests. This means breakpoints in production code are also hit when we run the tests.

> **Tip**
> To learn more about the debugger, search for lldb in the Apple documentation.

For now, keep the typo in the expected string constant as it is, but remove the breakpoint by dragging it with the mouse from the area to the left of the editor.

A breakpoint that breaks on test failure

Xcode has a built-in breakpoint that breaks on test failures. When this breakpoint is set, the execution of the tests is stopped, and a debug session is started whenever a test fails.

Usually, this is not what you want because in TDD, failing tests are normal and you don't need a debugger to find out what's going on. You explicitly wrote the test to fail at the beginning of the TDD workflow cycle.

But in case you need to debug one or more failing tests, it's good to know how this breakpoint is activated. Open the breakpoint navigator:

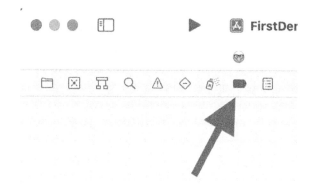

Figure 3.11 – The breakpoint navigator

At the bottom of the navigator view is a button with a plus sign (+). Click on it, and select **Test Failure Breakpoint**:

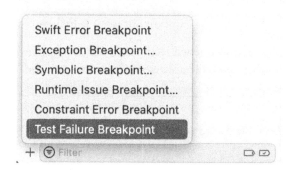

Figure 3.12 – Select Test Failure Breakpoint

As the name suggests, this breakpoint stops the execution of the tests whenever a test fails. We still have a failing test in our example. Run the tests to see the breakpoint in action.

The debugger stops at the line with the assertion because the tests fail. Like in the preceding example, you get a debug session so that you can put in LLDB commands to find out why the test failed.

Remove the breakpoint again because it's not very practical while performing TDD. In TDD, we have failing tests all the time. A test failure breakpoint would disturb the TDD flow too much.

The test again feature

Now, let's fix the error in the tests and learn how to run the previous test again. Open `FirstDemoTests.swift` and run only the failing test by clicking on the diamond symbol next to the test method. The test still fails. Fix it by changing the last character in `ContextuaI` to "l" in the `expected` string constant. Then, go to **Product | Perform Action | Test "test_makeHeadline_shouldCapitalisePassedInString_2()" Again**, or use the shortcut ^⌥⌘G to run just the previous test again. The shortcut is especially useful when you are working on one specific feature and you need to test whether the implementation is sufficient already.

Summary

In this chapter, we explored how unit testing and TDD works in Xcode. We saw real tests testing real code. Using the different test-related features of Xcode, we learned to write, run, and fix tests and to find test-relevant information. All this is important for the rest of the book. We need to know how to use Xcode when doing TDD.

In the next chapter, we will figure out the app we are going to build using test-driven development.

Exercises

1. Write a test for a method that reverses a string. Write the code that makes the test pass.

2. Write a test for a method that takes a headline and creates a filename from it. In the filename, make sure that spaces are replaced by _ and it only contains lowercase characters.

Section 2 – The Data Model

In most projects, the model layer is the part that is easiest to test. As we are just getting started, writing tests for model objects helps us to get into a testing mode mindset.

In this section, we will cover the following chapters:

- *Chapter 4, The App We Are Going to Build*
- *Chapter 5, Building a Structure for ToDo Items*
- *Chapter 6, Testing, Loading, and Saving Data*

4
The App We Are Going to Build

In the previous chapters, you learned how to write unit tests and saw an easy example of **test-driven development** (**TDD**). When starting TDD, writing unit tests is easy for most people. The hard part is transferring knowledge from writing tests to driving development. What can be assumed? What should be done before we write the first test? What should be tested to end up with a complete app?

As a developer, you are used to thinking in terms of code. When you see a feature on the requirement list for an app, your brain already starts to lay out the code for this feature. For recurring problems in iOS development (such as building table views), you most probably have already developed your own best practices.

In TDD, you should not think about the code while working on the test. The tests have to describe what the unit under test should do and not how it should do it. It should be possible to change the implementation without breaking the tests. Thinking like this is the hard part of TDD. You'll need practice before this becomes natural.

To practice this development approach, we will develop a simple to-do list app in the remainder of this book. It is, on purpose, a boring and easy app. We want to concentrate on the TDD workflow, not complex implementations. An interesting app would distract from what is important in this book—how to perform TDD.

This chapter introduces the app we are going to build and shows the views that the finished app will have.

These are the main topics of this chapter:

- A list of to-do items

- A view for the details of a to-do item

- A view to add to-do items

- The structure of the app

- Getting started in Xcode

Technical requirements

All the code in this chapter is uploaded (in complete form) here:

```
https://github.com/PacktPublishing/Test-Driven-iOS-
Development-with-Swift-Fourth-Edition/tree/main/chapter04
```

A list of to-do items

When starting the app (the one we are going to build), the user sees a list of to-do items on the screen of their iOS device. The items in the list consist of a title, an optional location, and the due date. New items can be added to the list by using an add (+) button, which is shown in the navigation bar of the view. The task list view will look like this:

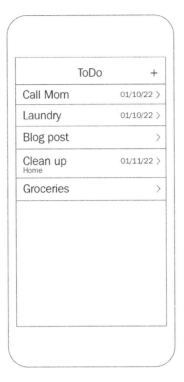

Figure 4.1 – A list of to-do items

As a user, I have the following requirements:

- I want to see a list of to-do items when I open the app.
- I want to add to-do items to the list.

In a to-do list app, the user will obviously need to be able to check off items when they are finished. The checked items are shown below the unchecked items, and it is possible to uncheck them again. The app uses the **Delete** button in the UI of the table view to check and uncheck items. Checked items will be put at the end of the list in a section with the **Done** header. The UI for the to-do item list will look like this:

Figure 4.2 – To-do items can be checked as Done

As a user, I have the following requirements:

- I want to check a to-do item to mark it as finished.
- I want to see all the checked items following the unchecked items.
- I want to uncheck a to-do item.
- I want to delete all the to-do items.

When the user taps an entry, the details of this entry are shown in the task detail view.

A view for the details of a to-do item

The task detail view shows all the information that's stored for a to-do item. The information consists of a title, due date, location (name and address), and a description. If an address is given, a map with an address is shown. The detail view also allows checking off the item as done. The **Details** view looks like this:

Figure 4.3 – The view for the details of a to-do item

As a user, I have the following requirements:

- I have tapped a to-do item in the list and I want to see its details.

- I want to check a to-do item from its details view.

You need to be able to add to-do items to the list. The next section shows what this input view will look like.

A view to add to-do items

When the user selects the add (+) button in the list view, the task input view is shown. The user can add information for the task. Only the title is required. The **Save** button can only be selected when a title is given. It is not possible to add a task that is already on the list. The **Cancel** button dismisses the view. The task input view will look like this:

Figure 4.4 – The view to add a to-do item to the list

As a user, I have the following requirements:

- Given that I tapped the add (+) button in the item list, I want to see a form to put in the details (title, optional date, optional location name, optional address, and optional description) of a to-do item.

- I want to add a to-do item to the list of to-do items by tapping on the **Save** button.

We will not implement the editing and deletion of tasks, but when you have worked through this book completely, it will be easy for you to add this feature yourself by writing the tests first.

Keep in mind that we will not test the look and design of the app. Unit tests cannot figure out whether an app looks like it was intended. Unit tests can test features, and these are independent of their presentation. In principle, it would be possible to write unit tests for the position and color of UI elements, but such things are very likely to change a lot in the early stages of development. We do not want to have failing tests only because a button has moved 10 points.

However, we will test whether the UI elements are present in the view. If your user cannot see the information for the tasks or if it is not possible to add all the information of a task, then the app does not meet the requirements.

In the next section, we will discuss the structure of the app we are going to build.

The structure of the app

Before we start to implement the different views of our to-do app, we need to think about the structure of our app. The app is quite simple on purpose to help keep the focus on the main topic of this book: building an app using TDD.

The table view controller, the delegate, and the data source

In iOS apps, data is often presented using a table view. Table views are highly optimized for performance; they are easy to use and implement. We will use a table view for the list of to-do items.

A table view is usually represented by `UITableViewController`, which is also the data source and delegate for the table view. This often leads to a massive table view controller, because it is doing too much: presenting the view, navigating to other view controllers, and managing the presentation of the data in the table view.

To reduce the responsibility of the table view controller a bit, we will use the coordinator pattern. This way, a coordinator is responsible for navigating between different views of the app. As our app is quite simple, we will only need one coordinator for the whole app.

The communication between the table view controller and the coordinator class will be defined using a protocol. Protocols define what the interface of a class looks like. This has a great benefit: if we need to replace an implementation with a better version (maybe because you have learned how to implement the feature in a better way), we only need to develop against the clear **application programming interface** (**API**). The inner workings of other classes do not matter.

Table view cells

As you can see in the preceding screenshots, the to-do list items have a title and, optionally, they can have a due date and a location name. The table view cells should only show the set data. We will accomplish this by implementing our own custom table view cell.

The model

The model of the app consists of the to-do item, the location, and an item manager, which allows the addition and removal of items and is also responsible for managing the items. Therefore, the controller will ask the item manager for items to present. The item manager will also be responsible for storing the items on disk.

Beginners often tend to manage the model objects within the controller. Then, the controller has a reference to a collection of items, and the addition and removal of items are directly done by the controller. This is not recommended because if we decide to change the storage of items (for example, using core data), their addition and removal would have to be changed within the controller. It is difficult to keep an overview of such a class as it does many different unrelated things; for this reason, it can be a source of bugs.

It's much easier to have a clear interface between the controller and the model objects because if we need to change how the model objects are managed, the controller can stay the same. We could even replace the complete model layer if we just keep the interface the same. Later in the book, we will see that this decoupling also helps to make testing easier.

Other views

The app will have two more views: a task detail view and a task input view.

When the user taps a to-do item in the list, the details of the item are presented in the task detail view controller. From the **Details** screen, the user will be able to check an item.

New to-do items will be added to the list through an input view. This view will be implemented using SwiftUI.

The development strategy

In this book, we will build the app from the inside out. We will start with the model and then build the controllers and networking. At the end of the book, we will put everything together.

Usually, you would rather build apps feature-by-feature when doing TDD, but by separating based on layers instead of features, it is easier to follow and keep an overview of what is happening. When you later need to refresh your memory, the relevant information you need is easier to find.

In the next section, we are going to set up the app in Xcode and tweak some Xcode behaviors.

Getting started in Xcode

Now, let's start our journey by creating a project that we will implement using TDD. Proceed as follows:

1. Open Xcode and create a new iOS project using the **App** template.

2. In the **Options** window, add `ToDo` as the product name, select the `Storyboard` interface and `Swift` as the language, and check the box next to **Include Tests**. Let the **Use Core Data** box stay unchecked.

   Xcode creates a small iOS project with three targets: one for the implementation code, one for the unit, and one for the UI tests. The template contains code that presents a single view on the screen.

3. To take a look at how the app target and test target fit together, select the project in the project navigator and then select the ToDoTests target. In the **General** tab, you'll find a setting for the **Host Application** that the test target should be able to test. It looks like this:

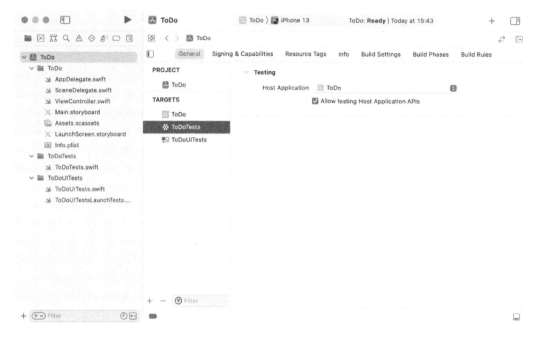

Figure 4.5 – General settings for the test target

Xcode has already set up the test target correctly to allow the testing of the implementations that we will write to the app target.

4. Unfortunately, Xcode also created a test target for UI tests. UI tests are too slow for TDD. To keep the feedback from the test running fast, we need to disable the UI tests for the main scheme. Click the scheme in the **Build** information bar at the top of the Xcode window and select the **Test** stage. Next, uncheck the box next to the UI test target. The process is illustrated in the following screenshot:

Figure 4.6 – Disabling the UI tests

Setting up useful Xcode behaviors for testing

Xcode has a feature called **Behaviors**. With the use of behaviors and tabs, Xcode can show useful information depending on its state.

Open the **Behaviors** window by navigating to **Xcode | Behaviors | Edit Behaviors**. On the left-hand side are the different stages for which you can add behaviors (**Build**, **Testing**, **Running**, and so on). These behaviors are useful when doing TDD.

The behaviors shown here are those that I find useful. Play around with the settings to find the ones most useful for you. Overall, I recommend using behaviors because I think they speed up development.

Useful build behaviors

When the building starts, Xcode compiles the files and links them together. To see what is going on, you can activate the **Build** log when the building starts. It is recommended that you open the **Build** log in a new tab because this allows you to switch back to the code editor when no error occurs during the build:

1. Select the **Starts** stage and check **Show** for **window tab**.

2. Put the name Log into the **named** field or use an emoji.

3.   Check **Show** for **navigator** and **Issues**.

4.   At the bottom of the window, check **Navigate to** and select **current log**. After you have made these changes, the settings window will look like this:

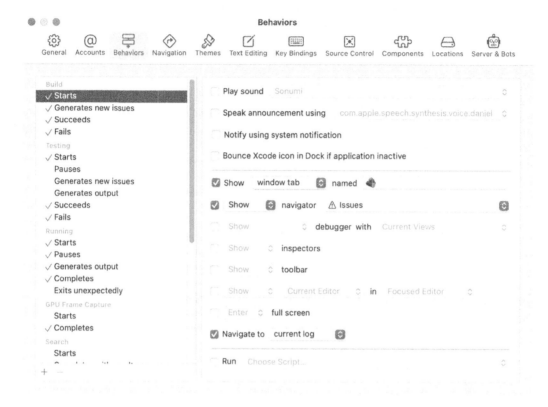

Figure 4.7 – Behavior to show the build log when building starts

5.   Build and run to see what the behavior looks like.

Testing behaviors

I have a window tab for coding. The name of this tab is 😀. Usually, in this tab, the test is open on the left-hand side, and in the **Assistant Editor** is the code to be tested (or in the case of TDD, the code to be written). It looks like this:

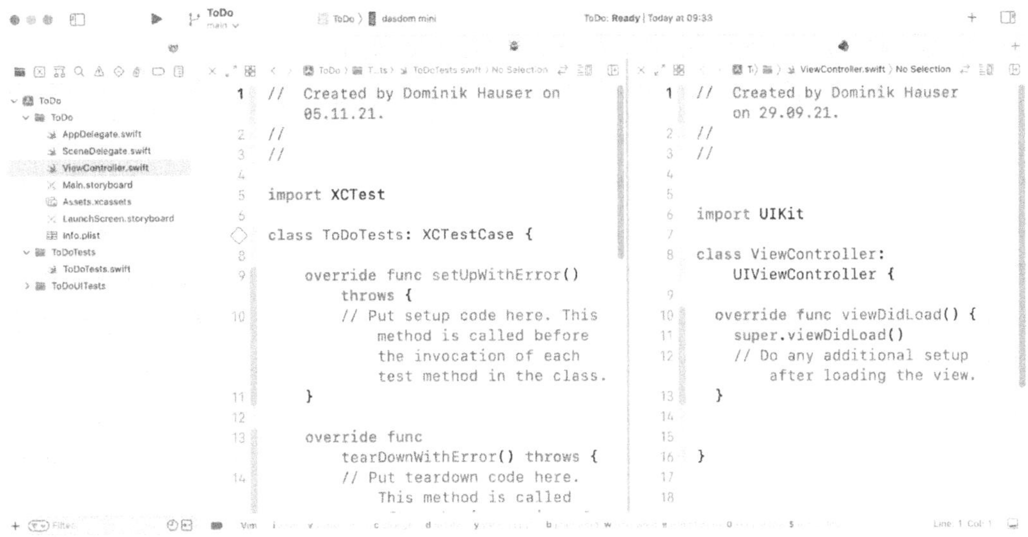

Figure 4.8 – The 🤓 tab

When the test starts, we want to see the code editor again. So, we add a behavior to show the 🤓 tab. In addition to this, we want to see the **Test** navigator and debugger with the console view.

When the test succeeds, Xcode should show a bezel to notify us that all tests have passed. Navigate to the **Testing | Succeeds** stage and check the **Notify using system notification** setting. In addition to this, it should hide the navigator and the debugger, because we want to concentrate on refactoring or writing the next test.

In case the testing fails (which happens a lot in TDD), Xcode should show a notification again. I like to hide the debugger because usually, it is not the best place to figure out what is going on in the case of a failing test. In most cases in TDD, we already know what the problem is.

You can even make your Mac speak announcements. Check **Speak announcements using** and select the voice you like but be careful not to annoy your co-workers. You might need their help in the future.

Now, the project and Xcode are set up, and we can start our TDD journey.

Summary

In this chapter, we took a look at the app that we are going to build throughout the course of this book. We took a look at how the screens of the app will look when we are finished with it. We created a project that we will use later on and learned about Xcode behaviors.

In the next chapter, we will develop the data model of the app using TDD. We will use structs for the model wherever we can because models are best represented in Swift by value types.

Exercises

1. Replicate the mock-up screens using a storyboard in Xcode.
2. Change the behaviors such that you can figure out if a test failed or if all tests passed without looking at the screen.

5
Building a Structure for ToDo Items

iOS apps are often developed using a design pattern called **Model-View-Controller** (**MVC**). In this pattern, each class, struct, or enum is either a model object, view, or controller. Model objects are responsible for storing data. They should be independent of the kind of presentation provided by the UI. For example, it should be possible to use the same model object for an iOS app and a command-line tool on macOS.

View objects present the data. They are responsible for making the objects visible (or hearable, in the case of a VoiceOver-enabled app) for the user. Views are special for the device that the app is executed on. In the case of a cross-platform app, view objects cannot be shared. Each platform needs an implementation of a view layer.

Controller objects communicate between the model and view objects. They are responsible for making the model objects presentable.

We will use MVC for our to-do app because it is one of the easiest design patterns, and it is commonly used by Apple in its sample code.

This chapter starts our journey in the field of TDD with the model layer of our app. By the end of this chapter, we will have a structure where we can store all the information about a to-do item, including an optional location.

In this chapter, we will cover the following topics:

- Implementing the ToDoItem struct
- Implementing the Location struct

Technical requirements

All the code for this chapter can be found (in its complete form) here: `https://github.com/PacktPublishing/Test-Driven-iOS-Development-with-Swift-Fourth-Edition/tree/main/chapter05`.

Implementing the ToDoItem struct

To be useful, to-do items need a minimal set of information. In this section, we will create a structure to hold this information while using tests to guide their development.

A to-do app needs a model class/struct to store information for to-do items:

1. We will start by adding a new test case to the unit test target. Open the to-do project that we created in the *Getting started with Xcode* section of *Chapter 4, The App We Are Going to Build*, and select the **ToDoTests** group.

2. Go to **File | New | File...**, navigate to **iOS | Source | Unit Test Case Class**, and click on **Next**. Put in the name `ToDoItemTests`, make it a subclass of `XCTestCase`, select **Swift** as the language, and click on **Next**.

3. In the next window, click on **Create**.

4. Now, delete the `ToDoTests.swift` template test case.

Adding a title property

A to-do item needs a `title`. Follow these steps to add one to our `ToDoItem` struct:

1. Open `ToDoItemTests.swift` and add the following import expression right below `import XCTest`:

```
@testable import ToDo
```

This is needed to be able to test the ToDo module. The `@testable` keyword makes the internal methods of the ToDo module accessible to the test case. Alternatively, you could make the methods accessible from the test target using the `public` or `open` access levels. But you should only do that when you need that access levels because, for example, the method is part of a Swift package.

2. Remove the two template test methods, `testExample()` and `testPerformanceExample()`.

3. The `title` string of a to-do item is required. Let's write a test to ensure that an initializer exists that will take a `title` string. Add the following test method to the end of the test case (but within the `ToDoItemTests` class):

```
// ToDoItemTests.swift
func test_init_takesTitle() {
    ToDoItem(title: "Dummy")
}
```

4. The static analyzer that's built into Xcode will complain that it `Cannot find 'ToDoItem' in scope`:

```
     func test_init_takesTitle() {
20       ToDoItem(title: "Dummy")        ⊗  Cannot find 'ToDoItem' in scope
21   }
```

Figure 5.1 – Xcode telling us that it cannot find the ToDoItem type

We cannot compile this code because Xcode cannot find the `ToDoItem` type. A non-compiling test is a failing test; as soon as we have a failing test, we need to write implementation code to make the test pass.

5. To add a file for the implementation code, first, click on the **ToDo** group in the **Project** navigator. Otherwise, the added file will be put into the test group.

6. Go to **File | New | File...**, navigate to the **iOS | Source | Swift File** template, and click on **Next**. In the **Save As** field, add the name ToDoItem.swift, make sure that the file is added to the ToDo target and not to the ToDoTests target, and click on **Create**:

Figure 5.2 – Adding the file to the main target

7. Open ToDoItem.swift in the editor and add the following code:

```
// ToDoItem.swift
struct ToDoItem {
}
```

This code is a complete implementation of a struct named ToDoItem. So, Xcode should now be able to find the ToDoItem identifier.

8. Run the test by either going to **Product | Test** or using the ⌘U shortcut. The code does not compile because an argument is being passed to a call that takes no arguments. This means that at this stage, we could initialize an instance of ToDoItem, like this:

```
let item = ToDoItem()
```

9. However, we want to have an initializer that takes a title. We need to add a property, named `title`, of the `String` type to store the `title` string:

```
// ToDoItem.swift
struct ToDoItem {
    let title: String
}
```

Run the test again; it will pass. We have implemented the first microfeature of our to-do app using TDD – and it wasn't even hard. For the rest of this book, we will do this over and over again until the app is complete. But first, we need to check whether there is anything to refactor in the existing test and implementation code. The tests and code are clean and simple, so there is nothing to refactor yet.

> **Tip**
>
> Always remember to check whether refactoring is needed once you have made the tests green.

There are, however, a few things to note about the test. First, Xcode shows a warning stating **Result of 'ToDoItem' initializer is unused**. To make this warning go away, assign the result of the initializer to an underscore; that is, `_ = ToDoItem(title: "Foo")`. This tells Xcode that we know what we are doing. We want to call the initializer of `ToDoItem`, but we do not care about its return value.

Second, there is no `XCTAssert` function call in the test. To add an assert, we could rewrite the test like this:

```
func test_init_takesTitle() {
    let item = ToDoItem(title: "Dummy")
    XCTAssertNotNil(item, "item should not be nil")
}
```

But in Swift, a non-failable initializer cannot return `nil`. It always returns a valid instance. This means that the `XCTAssertNotNil()` method is useless. We do not need it to ensure that we have written enough code to implement the tested microfeature. It is not needed to drive the development, and it does not make the code better.

Before we proceed with the next few tests, let's set up the editor in a way that makes the TDD workflow easier and faster. First, open ToDoItemTests.swift in the editor. Then, open the **Project** navigator and hold down the *Option* key while clicking on ToDoItem.swift to open it in the Assistant Editor. Depending on the size of your screen and your preferences, you may prefer to hide the navigator again. With this setup, you have the tests and the code side by side, and switching from test to code and vice versa takes no time at all. In addition to this, since the relevant test is visible while you write the code, it can guide the implementation.

Adding an itemDescription property

A to-do item can have a description. We would like to have an initializer that also takes a description string. Let's get started:

1. To drive the implementation, we need a failing test for the existence of this initializer:

    ```
    // ToDoItemTests.swift
    func test_init_takesTitleAndDescription() {
        _ = ToDoItem(title: "Dummy",
                itemDescription: "Dummy Description")
    }
    ```

    Again, this code does not compile because there is an extra argument called itemDescription in the call.

2. To make this test pass, we must add an itemDescription property of the String? type to ToDoItem:

    ```
    // ToDoItem.swift
    struct ToDoItem {
        let title: String
        let itemDescription: String?
    }
    ```

3. Run the tests. The `test_init_takesTitle()` test will fail (that is, it will not compile) because there is a **Missing argument for parameter 'itemDescription' in call**. The reason for this is that we use a feature of Swift where structs have an automatic initializer with arguments defining their properties. The initializer in the first test only has one argument, so the test fails. To make the two tests pass again, we need to add an initializer that can take a variable number of parameters. Swift functions (and `init` methods as well) can have default values for parameters. You will use this feature to set `itemDescription` to `nil` if there is no parameter for it in the initializer.

4. Add the following code to `ToDoItem`:

```
// ToDoItem.swift
init(title: String,
     itemDescription: String? = nil) {

    self.title = title
    self.itemDescription = itemDescription
}
```

This initializer has two arguments. The second argument has a default value, so we do not need to provide both arguments. When the second argument is omitted, the default value is used.

5. Now, run the tests to make sure that both tests pass.

Removing a hidden source of bugs

To be able to use a short initializer by only setting the title, we need to define it ourselves. But this also introduces a new source of potential bugs. We can remove the two microfeatures we have implemented and still have both tests pass. To take a look at how this works, open `ToDoItem.swift` and comment out the properties and assignment in the initializer:

```
struct ToDoItem {
//   let title: String
//   let itemDescription: String?

    init(title: String,
         itemDescription: String? = nil) {
```

```
//      self.title = title
//      self.itemDescription = itemDescription
    }
}
```

Run the tests. Both tests will still pass. The reason for this is that they do not check whether the values of the initializer arguments are set to any ToDoItem properties. We can easily extend the tests to make sure that the values are set. First, let's change the name of the first test to test_init_whenGivenTitle_setsTitle() and replace it with the following code:

```
// ToDoItemTests.swift
func test_init_whenGivenTitle_setsTitle() {
    let item = ToDoItem(title: "Dummy")
    XCTAssertEqual(item.title, "Dummy")
}
```

This test does not compile because ToDoItem does not have a title property (it is commented out). This shows that the test is now testing our intention. Remove the comment signs for the title property and assignment of the title in the initializer, and then run the tests again. All the tests will pass. Now, replace the second test with this one:

```
// ToDoItemTests.swift
func test_init_whenGivenDescription_setsDescription() {
    let item = ToDoItem(title: "Dummy",
                        itemDescription: "Dummy Description")
    XCTAssertEqual(item.itemDescription, "Dummy Description")
}
```

Remove the remaining comment signs in ToDoItem and run the tests again. Both the tests will pass again, and they now test that the initializer works.

> **Tip**
>
> It is a good idea to use speaking test method names – that is, names that tell the
> story of the test. It's quite common to use a pattern such as `test_<method
> name>_<precondition>_<expected behavior>`. This way, the
> method name tells all that you need to know about the test when a test fails.
> In this book, we will try to follow this pattern, but we will leave out some
> information (for example, the precondition) when the code gets harder to read
> because of the limited space we have. You should develop a pattern and use it
> in all your tests.

Adding a timestamp property

A to-do item can also have a due date represented by a `timestamp` property:

1. Add the following test to make sure we can initialize an instance of `ToDoItem`
    with `timestamp`:

    ```swift
    // ToDoItemTests.swift
    func test_init_setsTimestamp() {
        let dummyTimestamp: TimeInterval = 42.0
        let item = ToDoItem(title: "Dummy",
                            timestamp: dummyTimestamp)

        XCTAssertEqual(item.timestamp, dummyTimestamp)
    }
    ```

    Again, this test does not compile because there is an extra argument in the
    initializer. From the implementation of the other properties, we know that we have
    to add a `timestamp` property in `ToDoItem` and set it in the initializer.

2. Change `ToDoItem` so that it looks like this:

    ```swift
    // ToDoItem.swift
    struct ToDoItem {
        let title: String
        let itemDescription: String?
        let timestamp: TimeInterval?
    ```

```
init(title: String,
        itemDescription: String? = nil,
        timestamp: TimeInterval? = nil) {

    self.title = title
    self.itemDescription = itemDescription
    self.timestamp = timestamp
    }
}
```

3. Run the tests. With a bit of luck, all the tests will pass. But what happens if they don't pass on your computer? The reason for this may be because we compare two `TimeInterval` structures using `XCTAssertEqual(_:_:)`. `TimeInterval` is a type alias for `Double`. Doubles are floating-point numbers and as such are hard to compare to each other. Usually, you can't tell if two floating-point numbers are equal. You can only tell if they are equal in respect to some accuracy. That's why `XCTest` provides an assert method with accuracy.

4. Replace the assert method call in `test_init_setsTimestamp()` with the following method call:

```
XCTAssertEqual(item.timestamp!,
               dummyTimestamp,
               accuracy: 0.000_001)
```

Run the tests. You will see that all the tests pass.

You may have noticed that we have to force unwrap `item.timestamp` to use it in the assert method with accuracy. The reason for this is that, in contrast to `XCTAssertEqual(_:_:)`, `XCTAssertEqual(_:_:accuracy:)` can't compare optional values. `timestamp` in `ToDoItem` is optional so that to-do items without due dates can be created. Force unwrapping a value in a unit test is not as problematic as doing so in production code because a crash in a test is only visible for the developer.

But still, Apple added a feature to `XCTest` to deal with optional values better. This is so important for the rest of this book that it deserves a section to itself.

Dealing with optional values in unit tests

With Xcode 11, Apple introduced the XCTUnwrap(_:) function to XCTest. This function unwraps its parameter and returns the unwrapped value. If the parameter is nil, this function throws an error. In this section, we will use this function to improve our test code. Replace the test_init_setsTimestamp() test method with the following code:

```
// ToDoItemTests.swift
func test_init_setsTimestamp() throws {
  let dummyTimestamp: TimeInterval = 42.0
  let item = ToDoItem(title: "Dummy",
                      timestamp: dummyTimestamp)

  let timestamp = try XCTUnwrap(item.timestamp)
  XCTAssertEqual(timestamp,
                 dummyTimestamp,
                 accuracy: 0.000_001)
}
```

Several things have changed in this code. Let's look at them one by one:

- The method is now marked with throws. The reason for this is that we call a function that can throw an error. A test method that is marked with throws fails, when an error is thrown and not caught during its execution.

- With try XCTUnwrap(item.timestamp), we try to unwrap the item. timestamp value.

- The result is assigned to a variable that is used in the XCTAssertEqual method.

Whenever you have to deal with optionals in test code, this is the preferred way to do so. This way, you get the most valuable information in case the value is unexpectedly nil.

Adding a location property

The last property that we would like to be able to set in the initializer of ToDoItem is its Location. The location has a name and can optionally have a coordinate. We will use a struct to encapsulate this data into a type. Let's get started:

1. Add the following code to ToDoItemTests:

```
// ToDoItemTests.swift
func test_init_whenGivenLocation_setsLocation() {
    let dummyLocation = Location(name: "Dummy Name")
}
```

The test is not finished, but it already fails because Xcode **Cannot find 'Location' in scope**. There is no class, struct, or enum named Location yet.

2. Open the **Project** navigator and add a Swift file called Location.swift to the **ToDo** target. From our experience with the ToDoItem struct, we already know what is needed to make the test green.

3. Add the following code to Location.swift:

```
// Location.swift
struct Location {
    let name: String
}
```

This defines a struct called Location with a name property and makes the test code compilable again. But the test is not finished yet.

4. Add the following code to test_init_whenGivenLocation_setsLocation():

```
// ToDoItemTests.swift
func test_init_whenGivenLocation_setsLocation() {
    let dummyLocation = Location(name: "Dummy Name")
    let item = ToDoItem(title: "Dummy Title",
                        location: dummyLocation)

    XCTAssertEqual(item.location?.name,
                   dummyLocation.name)
}
```

Unfortunately, we cannot use the location itself to check for equality yet, so the following assert does not work:

```
XCTAssertEqual(item.location, dummyLocation)
```

The reason for this is that the first two arguments of XCTAssertEqual() have to conform to the Equatable protocol. We will add the protocol's conformance in the next chapter.

Again, this does not compile because the initializer of ToDoItem does not have an argument called Location.

5. Add the location property and initializer argument to ToDoItem. The result should look like this:

```swift
// ToDoItem.swift
struct ToDoItem {
    let title: String
    let itemDescription: String?
    let timestamp: TimeInterval?
    let location: Location?

    init(title: String,
         itemDescription: String? = nil,
         timestamp: TimeInterval? = nil,
         location: Location? = nil) {

        self.title = title
        self.itemDescription = itemDescription
        self.timestamp = timestamp
        self.location = location
    }
}
```

6. Run the tests again. All the tests will pass and there will be nothing to refactor. We have now implemented a struct to hold ToDoItem using TDD.

In the next section, we will implement a structure to store location data for to-do items.

Implementing the Location struct

In the previous section, we added a struct to hold information about the location. We will now add tests to make sure that Location has the required properties and initializer.

These tests could be added to ToDoItemTests, but they are easier to maintain when the test classes mirror the implementation classes/structs. So, we need a new test case class.

Open the **Project** navigator, select the ToDoTests group, and add a unit test case class called LocationTests. Make sure that you go to **iOS | Source | Unit Test Case Class** since we want to test the iOS code, and Xcode sometimes navigates to **OS X | Source**.

Set up the editor to show LocationTests.swift on the left-hand side and Location.swift in the Assistant Editor on the right-hand side. In the test class, add @testable import ToDo and remove the testExample() and testPerformanceExample() template tests.

Adding a coordinate property

The location of a to-do item will be used in the app to show a map in the details. A location on a map can be stored using latitude and longitude values. In the following steps, we will add a coordinate property to store this information:

1. To drive the addition of a Coordinate property, we need a failing test. For the coordinate, we will use the CLLocationCoordinate2D type from the Core Location framework.

2. Import CoreLocation below the existing import statements:

```
// LocationTests.swift
import XCTest
@testable import ToDo
import CoreLocation
```

3. Add the following test to LocationTests:

```
// LocationTests.swift
func test_init_setsCoordinate() throws {
    let coordinate = CLLocationCoordinate2D(latitude: 1,
                                            longitude: 2)
```

```
let location = Location(name: "",
                        coordinate: coordinate)

let resultCoordinate = try XCTUnwrap(location.
coordinate)
XCTAssertEqual(resultCoordinate.latitude, 1,
              accuracy: 0.000_001)
XCTAssertEqual(resultCoordinate.longitude, 2,
              accuracy: 0.000_001)
}
```

First, we created a coordinate and used it to create an instance of Location. Then, we asserted that the latitude and longitude values of the location coordinates have been set to the correct values. We use values of 1 and 2 in the initializer of CLLocationCoordinate2D because it also has an initializer that takes no arguments (CLLocationCoordinate2D()) and sets the longitude and latitude values to zero. We need to make sure that the initializer of Location assigns the coordinate argument to its property in the test.

> **Note**
>
> You may have noticed that we have omitted the message parameter in the XCTAssertEqual() function. This is because the used assertion already gives enough context to help us figure out what we expect in the test. We expect that the two values are the same. There is no need to duplicate that information in the message. If you find that information useful, feel free to add a message yourself.

The test does not compile because Location does not have a coordinate property yet. Similar to ToDoItem, we would like to have a short initializer for locations that only have a name argument. Therefore, we need to implement the initializer ourselves, and we cannot use the one provided by Swift.

4. Replace the contents of Location.swift with the following lines of code:

```
// Location.swift
import Foundation
import CoreLocation

struct Location {
    let name: String
```

```
let coordinate: CLLocationCoordinate2D?

init(name: String,
     coordinate: CLLocationCoordinate2D? = nil) {

    self.name = ""
    self.coordinate = coordinate
  }
}
```

5. Now, run the tests. All the tests will pass.

    Note that we have intentionally set name in the initializer to an empty string. This is the easiest implementation that makes the tests pass. But it is not what we want. The initializer should set the name of the location to the value in the name argument. So, we need another test to make sure that name is set correctly.

6. Add the following test to LocationTests:

```
// LocationTests.swift
func test_init_setsName() {
    let location = Location(name: "Dummy")

    XCTAssertEqual(location.name, "Dummy")
}
```

7. Run the test to make sure it fails. To make the test pass, change self.name = "" in the initializer of Location to self.name = name. Run the tests again to check whether they all pass now. There is nothing to refactor in the tests and their implementation.

Now, the Location structure can store a name and an optional coordinate to be used in the user interface of the app.

You may have asked yourself, why did we start with the coordinate property and not the name property when implementing that feature? We started with the coordinate because it was new terrain for us. We didn't know how to tackle testing Double values. Sometimes, it can be liberating to work on the most difficult problem first. It depends on how you write code. Tests help us make small baby steps and therefore help make difficult problems easier to solve.

I wanted to show you how to test the coordinate first, to address the elephant in the room. If you feel better when working on the easier tests first, go for it. But don't write unnecessary and easy tests just to procrastinate and avoid working on the hard ones.

Summary

In this chapter, we created a structure to hold information for to-do items using TDD. We learned that TDD means switching between test code and production code all the time. In addition, we realized that we should use the assert method with the accuracy parameter when we need to compare floating-point numbers. What you learned in this chapter will help you write better and more robust unit tests.

In the next chapter, we will build a structure to manage to-do items. They need to be stored somewhere and we need to have a way to add and check off to-do items.

Exercises

1. Try to write a test using `XCTAssertEqual(_:_:)` that fails, even if the values are equal, because of problems in comparing floating points. Hint: You often get this problem when using simple math functions such as addition and multiplication.

2. Make `ToDoItem` conform to `Equatable` and rewrite the assertions to take advantage of that conformance.

6
Testing, Loading, and Saving Data

At the moment, we have structures to hold the information of one to-do item. A usable to-do item app has to show and manage several to-do items. In addition, when the user closes the app and opens it again, they expect the to-do items to still be there.

This means our app needs structures that can store and load information of a list of to-do items.

In this chapter, we will add a class that stores and loads a list of to-do items to and from the filesystem of the iOS device. We will use the JSON format because it is a common choice in iOS development. It has the nice benefit in that it is easily readable by humans and computers.

The chapter is structured as follows:

- Publishing changes with Combine
- Checking items
- Storing and loading `ToDoItem`

Technical requirements

The source code for this chapter is available here: `https://github.com/` `PacktPublishing/Test-Driven-iOS-Development-with-Swift-Fourth-` `Edition/tree/main/chapter06`.

Publishing changes with Combine

In today's iOS apps, communication between different parts is often implemented using the **Combine** framework by Apple. In Combine, data changes are published and can be subscribed to. This design pattern helps to decouple the code and make it easier to maintain.

We will use Combine in our `ToDoItemStore` to inform, for example, the table view controller that something changed and the user interface should be updated with the new data.

Open Project Navigator and select the **ToDoTests** group. Go to the **iOS | Source | Unit Test Case** option to create a test case class with the name `ToDoItemStoreTests`. Import the `ToDo` module (`@testable import ToDo`) and remove the two test method templates.

Testing asynchronous Combine code

Up to now, all the code we've tested has been synchronous code. Publishing values in Combine is asynchronous. To be able to test Combine code, we need a way to halt the test and wait until the code we want to test is executed. `XCTest` provides `XCTestExpectation` for this task. Let's see how this works:

1. Add the following code to `ToDoItemStoreTests`:

    ```
    // ToDoItemStoreTests.swift
    func test_add_shouldPublishChange() {
        let sut = ToDoItemStore()
    }
    ```

    The **sut** abbreviation stands for **system under test**. We could also write this as `toDoItemStore`, but using `sut` makes it easier to read, and it also allows us to copy and paste test code into other tests when appropriate.

2. The test is not yet finished, but it already fails because Xcode cannot find
    `ToDoItemStore` in the scope. Open Project Navigator again and select
    the **ToDo** group. Go to **iOS | Source | Swift File**. This will create a Swift file;
    let's call it `ToDoItemStore.swift`. Add the following class definition to
    `ToDoItemStore.swift`:

```
// ToDoItemStore.swift
class ToDoItemStore {

}
```

This is enough to make the test code compilable.

3. Run the tests to make sure that they all pass and we can continue writing tests. Add
    the following code to `test_add_shouldPublishChange()`:

```
// ToDoItemStoreTests.swift
func test_add_shouldPublishChange() {
  let sut = ToDoItemStore()
  let publisherExpectation = expectation(
    description: "Wait for publisher in \(#file)"
  )
  var receivedItems: [ToDoItem] = []
  let token = sut.itemPublisher
}
```

First, we create an instance of `ToDoItemStore`. Next, we need an expectation to
wait for the asynchronous execution of our Combine code. With `description`,
we inform our future selves why we need this expectation. To figure out whether
`publisher` worked as expected, we need to subscribe to it in the test and check
the published value. We will store the value in the `receivedItems` variable.

The last line is the beginning of the subscription to the publisher, but we have
to pause before writing the rest because Xcode complains that **Value of type
'ToDoItemStore' has no member 'itemPublisher'**. This means we need to write
some code in the main target to make the test compile again.

4. First, we need to import the Combine framework. Then, we can add the publisher, like this:

```
// ToDoItemStore.swift
import Foundation
import Combine

class ToDoItemStore {
  var itemPublisher =
    CurrentValueSubject<[ToDoItem], Never>([])
}
```

If you haven't worked with Combine or Generics yet, this syntax might look a bit strange. `[ToDoItem]` in `<[ToDoItem], Never>` means that the publisher sends arrays of `ToDoItems`. The second part, `Never`, is the failure type of this publisher. `Never` means that this publisher cannot fail. In summary, `CurrentValueSubject<[ToDoItem], Never>([])` creates an instance of a `CurrentValueSubject` publisher that sends arrays of `ToDoItems` that never fail.

This fixes the error reported by the static analyzer. We can switch back to the test code.

5. Import Combine below the existing import statements and change the code in `test_add_shouldPublishChange()` so that it looks like this:

```
// ToDoItemStoreTests.swift
import Combine
// ...
func test_add_shouldPublishChange() {
  let sut = ToDoItemStore()
  let publisherExpectation = expectation(
    description: "Wait for publisher in \(#file)"
  )
  var receivedItems: [ToDoItem] = []
  let token = sut.itemPublisher
    .dropFirst()
    .sink { items in
      receivedItems = items
      publisherExpectation.fulfill()
```

```
        }

    let toDoItem = ToDoItem(title: "Dummy")
    sut.add(toDoItem)
    }
```

This does not compile. But before we switch back to the production code, let's see what we added here:

- First, we drop the first published value from `itemPublisher` using `dropFirst()`. We do this because a `CurrentValueSubject` publisher publishes the first current value as soon as we subscribe to it. But in the test, we only want to assert that the changes have been published.

- Next, we subscribe to the publisher using `sink(receiveValue:)`. The published value is passed into the `receivedValue` parameter. You can't see the parameter name in the code because we are using the trailing closure syntax as it is common in iOS development. We store the received value into the `receivedItems` variable. At this point, the asynchronous code we waited for in the test is finished. We tell the test runner that we don't need to wait any further by calling `fulfill()` on the expectation.

- The last two lines in this code are the execution of the method we want to test. We assume here that `ToDoItemStore` has an `add(_:)` method that allows us to add to-do items to the item store. As we haven't written this method yet, Xcode is complaining and we have to switch back to the production code. Follow the next step for that.

6. Add the following code to `ToDoItemStore`:

```
// ToDoItemStore.swift
func add(_ item: ToDoItem) {
}
```

This makes the test compilable again.

7. Switch back to the test code and add the last three lines in the following code to `test_add_shouldPublishChange()`:

```
// ToDoItemStoreTests.swift
func test_add_shouldPublishChange() {
    // ... arrange ...
```

```
    let toDoItem = ToDoItem(title: "Dummy")
    sut.add(toDoItem)


    wait(for: [publisherExpectation], timeout: 1)
    token.cancel()
    XCTAssertEqual(receivedItems.first?.title,
        toDoItem.title)
}
```

With `wait(for:timeout:)`, we tell the test runner to wait at this point until all expectations in the `first` parameter are fulfilled. If all the expectations are not fulfilled after the timeout has passed, the test fails. Next, we cancel the publisher. If we omitted this line, the compiler could remove the subscription because it looks like it is not used anywhere in the code. In the last line, we compare the received value with what we expect.

Finally, we can run the test. As expected, the test we just added fails because the publisher hasn't published anything yet.

We would like to use the assertion like this:
`XCTAssertEqual(receivedItems, [toDoItem])`. But this is not possible at the moment because `ToDoItem` does not conform to the `Equatable` protocol, which tells the compiler how to treat equality between two instances. We will fix that soon. But first, we need to make the tests green again.

8. Change the code in `ToDoItemStore` so that it looks like this:

```
// ToDoItemStore.swift
class ToDoItemStore {
  var itemPublisher =
    CurrentValueSubject<[ToDoItem], Never>([])
  private var items: [ToDoItem] = [] {
    didSet {
      itemPublisher.send(items)
    }
  }
}
```

```
func add(_ item: ToDoItem) {
    items.append(item)
  }
}
```

With this code, we added a `private` property to hold the to-do items in the item store. Whenever this property changes (for example, when a new item is added), it is published using the item publisher. As a result, in the `add(_:)` method, we only have to append the item to the items list.

9. Run the tests. All tests pass.

Now let's tackle the problem of `ToDoItem` not being equatable.

Making ToDoItem equatable

The step of making `ToDoItem` equatable is a refactoring step. Up to this point, the code worked without `ToDoItem` being equatable. But the readability of the test would greatly benefit if we could use `XCTAssertEqual` directly on an array of `ToDoItems`. The following steps show you how to do that:

1. First, add the `Equatable` protocol to the declaration of `ToDoItem`, like this:

```
// ToDoItem.swift
struct ToDoItem: Equatable {
  // ...
}
```

2. Next, do the same for the `Location` structure:

```
// Location.swift
struct Location: Equatable {
  // ...
}
```

3. Next, add the following method to the `Location` struct:

```
// Location.swift
static func == (lhs: Location, rhs: Location) -> Bool {
    if lhs.name != rhs.name {
        return false
    }
```

```
if lhs.coordinate == nil, rhs.coordinate != nil {
  return false
}
if lhs.coordinate != nil, rhs.coordinate == nil {
  return false
}
if let lhsCoordinate = lhs.coordinate,
    let rhsCoordinate = rhs.coordinate {
  if abs(lhsCoordinate.longitude -
    rhsCoordinate.longitude) > 0.000_000_1 {
    return false
  }
  if abs(lhsCoordinate.latitude -
    rhsCoordinate.latitude) > 0.000_000_1 {
    return false
  }
}
  return true
}
```

If Swift cannot automatically add `Equatable` conformance (for example, because one of the properties isn't `Equatable` itself), we need to add the `==` (`lhs:rhs:`) class method. The method looks a bit complicated but this is just because the `coordinate` property is optional. So, we also have to respect the cases when one coordinate is nil and the other isn't.

4. Now, go back to `test_add_shouldPublishChange()` and replace the assertion call at the end with this:

```
// ToDoItemStoreTests.swift
XCTAssertEqual(receivedItems, [toDoItem])
```

Run the tests. All tests pass. The assertion now looks way better and we assert exactly what we expect from the test. But the test is still hard to read. All that Combine code is distracting from the main objective of the test.

Let's add a helper function to the test case to improve the test code:

1. The helper function we are going to add is inspired by a `blog post` (https://www.swiftbysundell.com/articles/unit-testing-combine-based-swift-code/) by *John Sundell*. Add the following code at the end of `ToDoItemStoreTests.swift` but outside of the `ToDoItemStoreTests` class:

```swift
// ToDoItemStoreTests.swift
extension XCTestCase {
  func wait<T: Publisher>(
    for publisher: T,
    afterChange change: () -> Void) throws
    -> T.Output where T.Failure == Never {
    let publisherExpectation = expectation(
      description: "Wait for publisher in \(#file)"
    )
    var result: T.Output?
    let token = publisher
      .dropFirst()
      .sink { value in
        result = value
        publisherExpectation.fulfill()
      }

    change()
    wait(for: [publisherExpectation], timeout: 1)
    token.cancel()
    let unwrappedResult = try XCTUnwrap(
      result,
      "Publisher did not publish any value"
    )
    return unwrappedResult
  }
}
```

This code is similar to the code we wrote in `test_add_shouldPublishChange()`. It is modified a bit to make it work as an extension of `XCTestCase`.

2. Now, we can replace the test code with the following:

```swift
// ToDoItemStoreTests.swift
func test_add_shouldPublishChange() throws {
    let sut = ToDoItemStore()
    let toDoItem = ToDoItem(title: "Dummy")
    let receivedItems = try wait(for: sut.itemPublisher)
    {
        sut.add(toDoItem)
    }
    XCTAssertEqual(receivedItems, [toDoItem])
}
```

This change makes the test easy to understand. Run the tests again. All tests still pass.

> **Note**
>
> The `wait` method we just added to `XCTestCase` can throw an error. As a result, we had to add the `try` keyword to the call of this method. We could wrap the call in a `do-catch` block but there is a better way. When we mark the test method itself as `throws`, an error thrown during the test invocation is registered by the test runner as a test failure. This again makes the test easier to read and understand. During the course of this book, we will always use this feature of `XCTest` instead of writing `do-catch` blocks in test methods.

3. But how do we know that we didn't break the test? Let's make sure that the test can still fail. Go to `ToDoItemStore` and remove the `items.append(item)` line from `add(_:)`. Run the tests to make sure that the test we changed fails now.

4. But something is strange now. The test failure is shown as gray instead of red. The reason is that the failure is in the `wait` function we added to `XCTestCase`. To make the test failure be reported at the call site of that function, we need to change the function to this (we only show the relevant lines here):

```swift
// ToDoItemStoreTests.swift
extension XCTestCase {
    func wait<T: Publisher>(
        for publisher: T,
```

```
    afterChange change: () -> Void,
    file: StaticString = #file,
    line: Uint = #line) throws
  -> T.Output where T.Failure == Never {

    // …

    let unwrappedResult = try XCTUnwrap(
      result,
      "Publisher did not publish any value",
      file: file,
      line: line
    )
    return unwrappedResult
  }
}
```

The function now has two more parameters, file and line. They are set to the default values, #file and #line, respectively. These parameters are then used in the call to XCTUnwrap. When XCTUnwrap now fails, Xcode uses the file and line parameters to figure out where this function was called and reports the failure at the call site. Run the tests again to see the difference.

5. Then, make the test pass again by adding the line you deleted.

In the next section, we will implement an essential feature for a to-do list app: *checking items*.

Checking items

In a to-do app, the user needs to be able to mark to-do items as done. This is an important feature of a to-do app because part of the reason people use such apps is the satisfying feeling when marking a to-do as done.

So, our app also needs this feature. As the process of building this app is driven by tests, we start with a new test for this feature. But before we can add the test for this feature, we need to think about how we can assert in the test that the feature works. This means we need a way to get all the to-do items that are already done. The easiest way to differentiate the done to-do items from the ones that are still to be done is with a property in the to-do item itself. This way, we can filter all the to-do items according to the value of that property.

With this plan, we can start writing the test:

1. Add the following method to `ToDoItemStoreTests.swift`:

    ```
    // ToDoItemStoreTests.swift
    func test_check_shouldPublishChangeInDoneItems()
     throws {
       let sut = ToDoItemStore()
       let toDoItem = ToDoItem(title: "Dummy")
       sut.add(toDoItem)
       sut.add(ToDoItem(title: "Dummy 2"))
       let receivedItems = try wait(for: sut.itemPublisher) {
         sut.check(toDoItem)
       }
     }
    ```

    In the first four lines of this test, we set up `ToDoItemStore` with two to-do items. Next, we wait for the publisher and try to check the to-do item. Xcode tells us that the `check(_:)` method is missing. As the test code does not compile right now, we need to switch to the production code and add the `check(_:)` method.

2. Go to `ToDoItemStore.swift` and add the following method:

    ```
    // ToDoItemStore.swift
    func check(_ item: ToDoItem) {
    }
    ```

3. Run the tests to make the test code aware of this change. The test fails because the publisher does not publish anything when we call the `check(_:)` method. Change the code of the `check` method to the following:

    ```
    // ToDoItemStore.swift
    func check(_ item: ToDoItem) {
       items.append(ToDoItem(title: ""))
    }
    ```

    Wait a minute! This is not what the `check` method should do. Yes, you are right. This is just the simplest code that makes the test at this stage pass. In TDD, you should always write the simplest code that makes the test pass. If you know the code is wrong, you need to add more tests until the feature actually works.

4. Run the tests to confirm that all tests pass. Open `ToDoItemStore.swift` and change the code in `test_check_shouldPublishChangeInDoneItems()` such that it looks like this:

```swift
// ToDoItemStoreTests.swift
func test_check_shouldPublishChangeInDoneItems()
  throws {
    let sut = ToDoItemStore()
    let toDoItem = ToDoItem(title: "Dummy")
    sut.add(toDoItem)
    sut.add(ToDoItem(title: "Dummy 2"))

    let receivedItems = try wait(for: sut.itemPublisher)
    {
      sut.check(toDoItem)
    }

    let doneItems = receivedItems.filter({ $0.done })
    XCTAssertEqual(doneItems, [toDoItem])
}
```

The last two lines before the closing curly braces are new. In these two lines, we first filter all done to-do items, and then we assert that the result is an array with only the to-do item we checked.

5. The static analyzer of Xcode tells us that the `ToDoItem` type does not have a property with the name `done`. Open `ToDoItem.swift` and add this property:

```swift
// ToDoItem.swift
struct ToDoItem: Equatable {
  let title: String
  let itemDescription: String?
  let timestamp: TimeInterval?
  let location: Location?
  var done = false

  init(title: String,
       itemDescription: String? = nil,
       timestamp: TimeInterval? = nil,
```

```
      location: Location? = nil) {

   self.title = title
   self.itemDescription = itemDescription
   self.timestamp = timestamp
   self.location = location
  }
 }
```

Now, the code compiles again. Run the tests. The test_check_
shouldPublishChangeInDoneItems() test fails because the array with the
filtered items is empty. This is expected because the code we added to check(_:)
does not check any item. It just adds a new item with an empty title.

6. Go back to ToDoItemStore.swift. We need to replace the to-do item in the
   array with the one in which we changed the done property to true. Replace the
   check method with the following code:

```
// ToDoItemStore.swift
func check(_ item: ToDoItem) {
  var mutableItem = item
  mutableItem.done = true
  if let index = items.firstIndex(of: item) {
    items[index] = mutableItem
  }
}
```

First, we get a mutable copy of the item. Next, we change done to true and finally,
we replace the item in the items array with the changed item.

Even though this should make the test pass, it still fails. Click the red diamond next
to the failure message to expand it. Read the message carefully. The test fails because
the two arrays are not the same. The to-do item in the result array has another value
in the done property.

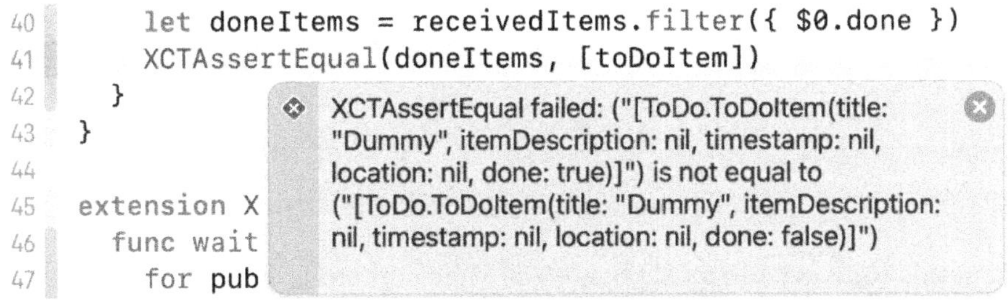

```
40      let doneItems = receivedItems.filter({ $0.done })
41      XCTAssertEqual(doneItems, [toDoItem])
42    }
43  }
44
45  extension X
46    func wait
47      for pub
```

⬦ XCTAssertEqual failed: ("[ToDo.ToDoItem(title: "Dummy", itemDescription: nil, timestamp: nil, location: nil, done: true)]") is not equal to ("[ToDo.ToDoItem(title: "Dummy", itemDescription: nil, timestamp: nil, location: nil, done: false)]") ⊗

Figure 6.1 – Expanded failure message telling us that the items are different

This makes sense. By adding the `done` property, we changed how Swift figures out whether two to-do items are the same. This is not what we want. A to-do item should have an identity.

7. Let's add a property that provides the to-do item with an identity. Open `ToDoItem.swift` and replace the `ToDoItem` structure with the following code:

```
// ToDoItem.swift
struct ToDoItem: Equatable {
  let id: UUID
  let title: String
  let itemDescription: String?
  let timestamp: TimeInterval?
  let location: Location?
  var done = false
  init(title: String,
       itemDescription: String? = nil,
       timestamp: TimeInterval? = nil,
       location: Location? = nil) {

    self.id = UUID()
    self.title = title
    self.itemDescription = itemDescription
    self.timestamp = timestamp
    self.location = location
  }
```

```swift
static func == (lhs: ToDoItem, rhs: ToDoItem) ->
Bool {
    return lhs.id == rhs.id
  }
}
```

With this code, we add an ID that is set when an item is created. In addition, we use this `id` property to figure out whether two to-do items are the same.

8. Run the tests. All tests pass.

9. Before we move on, we have to clean up the tests a bit. In the first line of each test, we create the system under test (`sut`). This code should be put into `setUpWithError()`. First, add the following property to `ToDoItemStoreTests`:

```swift
// ToDoItemStoreTests.swift
var sut: ToDoItemStore!
```

10. Next, change `setUpWithError()` and `tearDownWithError()` like this:

```swift
// ToDoItemStoreTests.swift
override func setUpWithError() throws {
  sut = ToDoItemStore()
}
override func tearDownWithError() throws {
  sut = nil
}
```

11. Now we can remove the following line of code from each of the tests:

```swift
let sut = ToDoItemStore()
```

This makes the tests easier to understand.

We can now add and check to-do items using our `ToDoItemStore`. But at the moment, the to-do items are only held in memory as long as the app runs. `ToDoItemStore` needs to store the to-do items somewhere and load them into memory as soon as the app starts again. In the next section, we will implement exactly this.

Storing and loading ToDoItems

To test storing and loading to-do items, we first need to create an instance of the `ToDoItemStore` class, add a to-do item, destroy that store instance, and create a new one. When we add a to-do item in the first instance, all items should be stored in the filesystem. When creating the second instance, the stored items should be loaded again from the filesystem. This means when we find the item we added in the first instance after we created the second instance, storing and loading works.

Implementing storing and loading

It is essential that the test controls the environment needed for itself. This means for storing and loading to-do items, the test needs to control where the items are stored. For example, if we used Core Data to persist the to-do items, the test would be responsible for setting up a fake Core Data store just used for the test. In our app, we will store the to-do items in a JSON file. So, the test needs to control where the JSON file is stored. Let's see how this can be done:

1. Add the following test method code to `ToDoItemStore`:

    ```
    // ToDoItemStoreTests.swift
    func test_init_shouldLoadPreviousToDoItems() {
      var sut1: ToDoItemStore? =
        ToDoItemStore(fileName: "dummy_store")
    }
    ```

    In this test, we don't use the instance created in `setUpWithError()` because we need to pass in the name of the store to be used. Xcode complains that we passed an argument to a call that takes no arguments. This means we have to pause writing the test code and switch to the production code.

2. Add the following initializer to `ToDoItemStore`:

    ```
    // ToDoItemStore.swift
    init(fileName: String = "todoitems") {
    }
    ```

This is enough to make the test compile again. This initializer allows passing the filename for the JSON file into `ToDoItemStore`. The `fileName` parameter has a default value because in the production code, the `ToDoItemStore` class should control where the file is stored.

3. Now we can write the rest of the test code:

```swift
// ToDoItemStoreTests.swift
func test_init_shouldLoadPreviousToDoItems() {
  var sut1: ToDoItemStore? =
    ToDoItemStore(fileName: "dummy_store")
  let publisherExpectation = expectation(
    description: "Wait for publisher in \(#file)"
  )

  let toDoItem = ToDoItem(title: "Dummy Title")
  sut1?.add(toDoItem)
  sut1 = nil
  let sut2 = ToDoItemStore(fileName: "dummy_store")
  var result: [ToDoItem]?
  let token = sut2.itemPublisher
    .sink { value in
      result = value
      publisherExpectation.fulfill()
    }

  wait(for: [publisherExpectation], timeout: 1)
  token.cancel()
  XCTAssertEqual(result, [toDoItem])
}
```

This code looks a bit intimidating, but it only contains concepts we've already covered. Let's go over that code step by step:

I.   We create an instance of `ToDoItemStore` and a test expectation.

II. Next, we add an item to the to-do item store and destroy the store by setting it to nil.

III. Then, we create a new to-do item store and subscribe to its `itemPublisher`. But this time, we do not drop the first published value from the publisher. As the publisher is a `CurrentValueSubject` structure, the subscriber receives the current value as soon as it subscribes to the publisher.

IV. Finally, we wait for the asynchronous execution of the Combine code and assert that the published items array contains the item we added to the initial to-do item store.

Run the tests. This test fails, because we haven't implemented storing and loading yet. Let's implement the code.

4. We need to store the filename in a property and access it when we store and load the items. Add the following property and change the initializer to set that property:

```swift
// ToDoItemStore.swift
private let fileName: String
init(fileName: String = "todoitems") {
  self.fileName = fileName
}
```

5. The next step is to make `ToDoItem` convertible to JSON format. Swift can do this for us if all the properties of a type are convertible to JSON. The only thing we as the developer have to do is to add the `Codable` protocol to the type. Change the declaration of `ToDoItem` such that it reads like this:

```swift
// ToDoItem.swift
struct ToDoItem: Equatable, Codable {
```

6. Xcode complains that **Type 'ToDoItem' does not conform to 'Decodable'**. The reason for this is that the `Location` property does not conform to `Codable` yet. Change the declaration of `Location` to the following:

```swift
// Location.swift
struct Location: Equatable, Codable {
```

Now Xcode tells us that `Location` does not conform to `Codable`. Oh, bummer! `CLLocationCoordinate2D` does not conform to `Codable`. We could implement the conformance ourselves, but there is an easier way. We create a `Coordinate` struct that serves the same purpose but is `Codable`. Create a new Swift file with the ⌘N shortcut and call it `Coordinate`. Set **Group** to **ToDo** and make sure that it is added to the **ToDo** target.

Figure 6.2 – Creating a file for the Coordinate structure

7. Add the following code to the new file:

```swift
// Coordinate.swift
struct Coordinate: Codable {
    let latitude: Double
    let longitude: Double
}
```

As Double is Codable, a structure only consisting of Double properties is also Codable.

8. Now we can replace the CLLocationCoordinate2D type in Location with our new Coordinate type:

```
// Location.swift
struct Location: Equatable, Codable {
  let name: String
  let coordinate: Coordinate?

  init(name: String,
       coordinate: Coordinate? = nil) {

    self.name = name
    self.coordinate = coordinate
  }
  // …
}
```

With this change, we no longer depend on Core Location and can remove its import from Location.swift.

We have changed some code. How do we make sure that everything we implemented before still works? With our tests! To do that, we first have to disable the currently failing test because of the incomplete implementation of storing and loading to-do items. We know that this test still fails because we are not finished with the implementation. We only want to run the tests that were green before we started implementing storing and loading. Let's get started:

1. Go to ToDoItemStoreTests and add the following call of XCTSkipIf(_:_:) at the beginning of the test. Note that you also have to add the throws keyword to the test signature:

```
// ToDoItemStoreTests.swift
func test_init_shouldLoadPreviousToDoItems() throws {
    try XCTSkipIf(true, "Just test Coordinate change")
    // …
}
```

With this call, we tell the test runner that it should skip this test. When we are done with the change of the coordinate type, we just have to remove this line of code to activate the test again.

2. Run the tests to figure out whether the coordinate change was successful or whether we missed something. The `test_init_setsCoordinate()` test does not compile because we changed the coordinate type. Replace the `CLLocationCoordinate2D` type with `Coordinate` and remove the import of `CoreLocation`:

```swift
// LocationTests.swift
func test_init_setsCoordinate() throws {
    let coordinate = Coordinate(latitude: 1,
        longitude: 2)
    let location = Location(name: "",
        coordinate: coordinate)
    let resultCoordinate = try
    XCTUnwrap(location.coordinate)
    XCTAssertEqual(resultCoordinate.latitude, 1,
        accuracy: 0.000_001)
    XCTAssertEqual(resultCoordinate.longitude, 2,
        accuracy: 0.000_001)
}
```

3. Run the tests again. Now all tests pass.

This is huge! For the first time, we used unit tests to make refactoring easier. We didn't have to check each and every file to see whether the coordinate property was used and whether we had to adapt the type. We just had to run the tests. Now imagine we're working on a code base with hundreds of thousands of lines of code. The confidence you gain with a good test suite makes refactoring code effortless.

Go back to `ToDoItemStoreTests` and remove the `XCTSkipIf(_:_:)` call. Run the tests to confirm that `test_init_shouldLoadPreviousToDoItems()` still fails.

Now that `ToDoItem` conforms to `Codable`, we can store a list of to-do items in a JSON structure:

1. Add the following method to `ToDoItemStore`:

```swift
// ToDoItemStore.swift
private func saveItems() {
    if let url = FileManager.default
        .urls(for: .documentDirectory,
                in: .userDomainMask)
```

```
        .first?
        .appendingPathComponent(fileName) {
    do {
      let data = try JSONEncoder().encode(items)
      try data.write(to: url)
    } catch {
      print("error: \(error)")
    }
  }
}
```

First, we get a file URL to store the JSON file to. Next, we get a Data object from the to-do items and write it to the file URL. As the conversion to JSON and writing to the file URL can throw an error, we embedded these calls into a do-catch block.

2. The items need to be saved whenever something in the list of to-do items changes. Change the add(_:) method such that it looks like this:

```
// ToDoItemStore.swift
func add(_ item: ToDoItem) {
  items.append(item)
  saveItems()
}
```

3. When we add a new item to the store, we save the list to the filesystem. We also need a method that loads the to-do items. Add the following method to ToDoItemStore:

```
// ToDoItemStore.swift
private func loadItems() {
  if let url = FileManager.default
      .urls(for: .documentDirectory,
              in: .userDomainMask)
      .first?
      .appendingPathComponent(fileName) {

    do {
      let data = try Data(contentsOf: url)
      items = try JSONDecoder()
```

```
            .decode([ToDoItem].self, from: data)
    } catch {
        print("error: \(error)")
    }
  }
}
```

This method is the reverse of the `saveItems` method. We get the same file URL in the beginning. Then, we load the data from the filesystem and convert it from the JSON format to a list of to-do items.

4. We call this method in the initializer of `ToDoItemStore`:

```
// ToDoItemStore.swift
init(fileName: String = "todoitems") {
    self.fileName = fileName
    loadItems()
}
```

That should make our test green. Run the tests to confirm.

Depending on your configuration, your tests might indeed be green. But most probably, some of the tests in `ToDoItemStoreTests` will fail. With storing and loading to-do items, the tests now depend on the tests that ran before. This is bad and should be avoided. When tests depend on the order in which they are executed, a test suite is not reliable. Tests can fail on some computers or in some environments. We need to fix this:

1. First, all tests should use a dummy JSON file. So, replace the setup code in `ToDoItemStoreTests` with this:

```
// ToDoItemStoreTests.swift
override func setUpWithError() throws {
    sut = ToDoItemStore(fileName: "dummy_store")
}
```

2. Second, we have to remove the JSON file after each test execution:

```
// ToDoItemStoreTests.swift
override func tearDownWithError() throws {
    sut = nil
    if let url = FileManager.default
        .urls(for: .documentDirectory,
```

```
                        in:  .userDomainMask)
        .first?
        .appendingPathComponent("dummy_store") {
      try? FileManager.default.removeItem(at: url)
    }
  }
```

I know what you are thinking. We used the code to get the file URL for the JSON file a third time. We should clean that up. No worries, we will do that next.

Run all tests twice. In the second run, all tests should be green.

Cleaning up the code

In software development, we should follow the DRY principle. **DRY** stands for **don't repeat yourself**. By copying the code that creates the file URL for the JSON file two times, we violated this principle. Let's make this code reusable.

Select the **ToDo** group in Project Navigator in Xcode and add a new Swift file (**iOS | Source | Swift File**). Call the file FileManagerExtension.swift and make sure it is added to the main target of our project.

Follow these steps to remove the duplicated code:

1. Add this extension to FileManagerExtension.swift:

```
// FileManagerExtension.swift
extension FileManager {
  func documentsURL(name: String) -> URL {
    guard let documentsURL = urls(for:
      .documentDirectory,
    in: .userDomainMask).first else {
      fatalError()
    }
    return documentsURL.appendingPathComponent(name)
  }
}
```

2. Open `ToDoItemStore.swift` and replace `saveItems()` with the
    following implementation:

```swift
// ToDoItemStore.swift
private func saveItems() {
    let url = FileManager.default
        .documentsURL(name: fileName)
    do {
        let data = try JSONEncoder().encode(items)
        try data.write(to: url)
    } catch {
        print("error: \(error)")
    }
}
```

> **Note**
>
> Usually, you wouldn't use the `FileManager` singleton directly here. In real
> code, you would rather pass in the kind of storage into the `ToDoItemStore`
> as a dependency using Dependency Injection. We take the approach above to
> keep the book as short as possible and to not distract from the main topic of
> this section.

3. Next, replace `loadItems()` with this code:

```swift
// ToDoItemStore.swift
private func loadItems() {
    let url = FileManager.default
        .documentsURL(name: fileName)
    do {
        let data = try Data(contentsOf: url)
        items = try JSONDecoder()
            .decode([ToDoItem].self, from: data)
    } catch {
        print("error: \(error)")
    }
}
```

4. Finally, replace `tearDownWithError()` in `ToDoItemStoreTests.swift` with the following code:

```swift
// ToDoItemStoreTests.swift
override func tearDownWithError() throws {
  sut = nil
  let url = FileManager.default
    .documentsURL(name: "dummy_store")
  try? FileManager.default.removeItem(at: url)
}
```

Run all tests to make sure they still pass.

5. We are not done yet. There is one test missing. When the user checks a to-do item as done, the list of items should also be written to the filesystem. To make sure that is the case, add the following test to `ToDoItemStoreTests.swift`:

```swift
func test_init_whenItemIsChecked_
  shouldLoadPreviousToDoItems() throws {
  var sut1: ToDoItemStore? =
  ToDoItemStore(fileName: "dummy_store")
  let publisherExpectation = expectation(
    description: "Wait for publisher in \(#file)"
  )

  let toDoItem = ToDoItem(title: "Dummy Title")
  sut1?.add(toDoItem)
  sut1?.check(toDoItem)
  sut1 = nil
  let sut2 = ToDoItemStore(fileName: "dummy_store")
  var result: [ToDoItem]?
  let token = sut2.itemPublisher
    .sink { value in
      result = value
      publisherExpectation.fulfill()
    }

  wait(for: [publisherExpectation], timeout: 1)
  token.cancel()
```

```
        XCTAssertEqual(result?.first?.done, true)
    }
```

This test looks kind of like `test_init_shouldLoadPreviousToDoItems()`. But here, we check `toDoItem` before we destroy the to-do item store. In addition, we assert at the end that the loaded to-do item is checked as done.

6. To make this test pass, add the call to `saveItems()` within the `if let` conditional of the `check(_:)` method:

```
func check(_ item: ToDoItem) {
  var mutableItem = item
  mutableItem.done = true
  if let index = items.firstIndex(of: item) {
    items[index] = mutableItem
    saveItems()
  }
}
```

Before you move on, make sure that all tests pass.

Summary

In this chapter, we have explored how to test Combine code. To make the tests easier to understand, we introduced a helper method and improved its failure message. We figured out how to make an `Equatable` type and how this can help in unit tests. Finally, we learned how to test storing and loading a JSON file to and from the filesystem of the iOS device.

With these skills, you should be able to write tests for a variety of different model scenarios.

In the next chapter, we will start building the user interface. We will start with the list of to-do items.

Exercises

1. Remove the expectation from the tests that test Combine code and check whether they fail.

2. Think about what needs to be done to check whether the stored file is indeed in JSON format. Do you think such a test is of any use?

Section 3 – Views and View Controllers

Testing views and view controllers is a bit more complicated. But, as you will see in this section, after you have practiced a bit, you will be able to write robust tests for user interfaces. For the tests of our SwiftUI code, we will get some help from a third-party library.

In this section, we will cover the following chapters:

- *Chapter 7, Building a Table View Controller for the To-Do Items*
- *Chapter 8, Building a Simple Detail View*
- *Chapter 9, Test-Driven Input View in SwiftUI*

7
Building a Table View Controller for the To-Do Items

If you have talked to other iOS developers about unit testing and the test-driven development of iOS apps, you might have heard the opinion that the user interface of iOS apps is not testable and also shouldn't be tested. Many developers state that it is enough to check whether the user interface is correct by running the app during development and testing it manually.

That might be true for the initial implementation of the user interface. During the development process, you run the app often on the iOS simulator or on your test devices and most bugs and errors in the user interface are quite obvious.

However, the main benefit of a user interface that is backed by unit tests is the ability to fearlessly refactor code that is no longer perfect. As a developer, you gain experience every day, and each year, Apple releases new APIs that make our code easier to understand and sometimes easier to write. Long-living apps need to be refactored all the time to keep them manageable.

This is the main argument for writing tests for user interfaces in iOS development. When you are confident that the user interface is backed by good tests, you can execute extreme refactoring without breaking tested features.

In this chapter, we are going to build a table view controller that shows the information of the to-do items. This view controller is the main part of the app, so it is a good idea to start with it. The chapter is structured as follows:

- Adding the table view for the to-do items

- Testing the data source of a table view

- Refactoring to a diffable data source

- Presenting two sections

- Implementing the delegate of a table view

After you have worked through this chapter, you will be able to write unit tests for table view controllers and table view cells.

Technical requirements

The source code for this chapter is available here: `https://github.com/PacktPublishing/Test-Driven-iOS-Development-with-Swift-Fourth-Edition/tree/main/chapter07`.

Adding the table view for the to-do items

As always, we start with a test. But before we can write the test, we need a new test class. Follow these steps to add a test class for the view controller that shows the to-do items:

1. Select the **ToDoTests** group in the Project navigator and add a new file from the **File** menu in Xcode. Select the template from **iOS | Source | Unit Test Case Class** and then click **Next**. Insert the name `ToDoItemsListViewControllerTests`.

2. In the created file, add `@testable import ToDo` and remove the two template test methods.

3. Add a property for the system under test (`sut`):

```
// ToDoItemsListViewControllerTests.swift
class ToDoItemsListViewControllerTests: XCTestCase {
```

```
    var sut: ToDoItemsListViewController!

    override func setUpWithError() throws {
        // Put setup code here. This ...
    }

    override func tearDownWithError() throws {
        // Put teardown code here. This ...
    }
}
```

Xcode complains that it **Cannot find type 'ToDoItemsListViewController' in scope**. This is expected as we haven't added this class yet.

4. Select the **ToDo** group in the Project navigator and add a new file through the **File** menu. Select the template from **iOS** | **Source** | **Cocoa Touch Class** and then click **Next**. Insert the name `ToDoItemsListViewController` in the **Class** field and make it a **Subclass of: UIViewController**. Make sure that **Also create XIB file** is not checked.

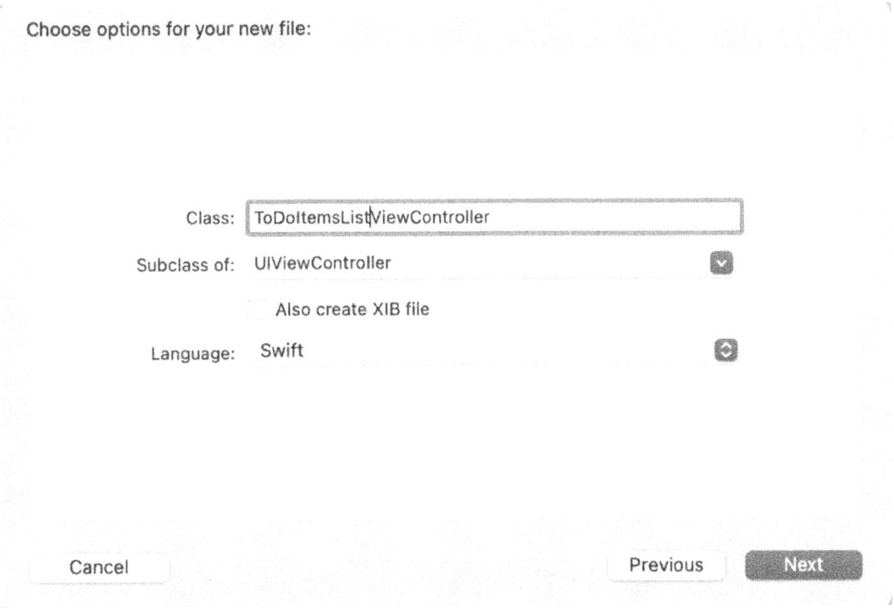

Choose options for your new file:

        Class: ToDoItemsListViewController

  Subclass of: UIViewController

             Also create XIB file

   Language: Swift

Cancel   Previous   Next

Figure 7.1 – Options for ToDoItemsListViewController

Remove all the template code within the `ToDoItemsListViewController` class.

5. We are going to switch between `ToDoItemsListViewController` and its test class several times. So, it might be a good idea to open both files side by side. In Xcode, you can do that by clicking the `ToDoItemsListViewControllerTests.swift` file in the Project navigator and then holding down the *Option* key and clicking the `ToDoItemsListViewController.swift` file. Xcode then opens the second file in the Assistant editor.

Figure 7.2 – Test code and production code side by side in Xcode

6. Before we can test anything in the view controller, we need to set up the system under test. Replace the `setUpWithError()` method with the following code:

```swift
// ToDoItemsListViewControllerTests.swift
override func setUpWithError() throws {
    let storyboard = UIStoryboard(name: "Main", bundle:
nil)
    sut = try XCTUnwrap(
        storyboard.instantiateInitialViewController()
        as? ToDoItemsListViewController
    )
    sut.loadViewIfNeeded()
}
```

As the view controller will be set up in the Main storyboard, we need to load it from the storyboard in the setup code. Note that the call to loadViewIfNeeded() is the actual loading of the view. If we don't call that method, the view does not get loaded and all outlets are nil.

7. To be a good citizen, we also need to clean up after each test. Replace the tearDownWithError() method with the following:

```
// ToDoItemsListViewControllerTests.swift
override func tearDownWithError() throws {
    sut = nil
}
```

Loading from a storyboard can go wrong. Let's add a test to make sure this works.

8. Add the following test to ToDoItemsListViewControllerTests:

```
// ToDoItemsListViewControllerTests.swift
func test_shouldBeSetup() {
    XCTAssertNotNil(sut)
}
```

This test asserts that the system under test is not nil after being loaded from the storyboard.

Run the tests to make sure that setting up the system under tests works. This test fails in setupWithError.

The setup method can't instantiate an instance of ToDoItemsListViewController from the storyboard because the initial view controller in the storyboard is of the ViewController type. Let's fix that.

9. Open **Main.storyboard** and change the **Class** field of the initial view controller to `ToDoItemsListViewController`.

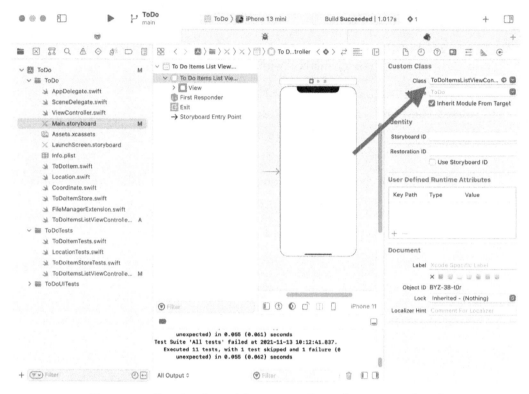

Figure 7.3 – Changing the initial view controller in the Main storyboard

Run the tests again to confirm that all the tests now pass.

Finally, we are ready to write the first test in this new test class. In the following steps, we add a test that asserts that the view controller has a `tableView` property for the to-do items. Let's go:

1. Add the following test method to `ToDoItemsListViewControllerTests`:

```swift
// ToDoItemsListViewControllerTests.swift
func test_shouldHaveTableView() {
    XCTAssertTrue(sut.tableView.isDescendant(of: sut.view))
}
```

The `isDescendant(of:)` method is defined on `UIView` and it returns `true` if the view on which it is called is in the hierarchy of the view that is passed in as a parameter. This means that this test asserts that `tableView` is added to `sut.view` or one of its subviews.

Xcode complains that a **Value of type 'ToDoItemsListViewController' has no member 'tableView'**. This is not a surprise because we haven't yet added a `tableView` property to `ToDoItemsListViewController`.

2. Open **Main.storyboard** in the interface builder and open the library by clicking the plus button in the toolbar and dragging a table view onto the view of the view controller.

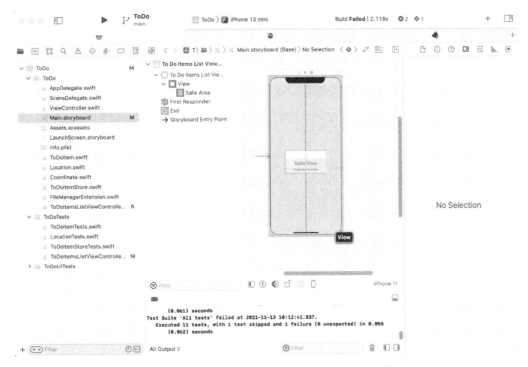

Figure 7.4 – Adding a table view to the view controller

3. Open the Assistant editor using the **Editor | Assistant menu item**, hold down the *Ctrl* key, and drag a connection from the table view into the `ToDoItemsListViewController` class.

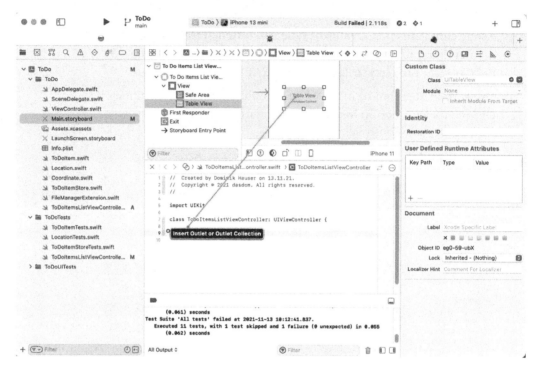

Figure 7.5 – Dragging a connection from the storyboard into the class

4. Set the name of this property to `tableView` and click **Connect**.

Run all the tests. All the tests pass. We have added a table view to the view of the view controller.

A table view is managed by a data source and a delegate. In the next section, we will implement parts of the data source of the table view.

Testing the data source of a table view

In this section, we will implement parts of the data source for the table view using test-driven development. We will use the traditional approach by using the view controller as the data source. In the next section, we will switch to a diffable data source. Our challenge in this section is to write the tests so that they are independent of the actual implementation of the data source.

But first, we need to talk about test doubles.

Adding a test double

In the film industry, doubles are used in scenes that are too dangerous for the actor. The double must look and act like the actor. In software testing, we have something similar: test doubles. Test doubles look and act like a piece of code, but can be controlled completely from within the test. For example, to test the data source of our table view, we need to connect the view controller with a store of to-do items. We could use the store we already implemented. But this would make the tests for the table view depend on the implementation of ToDoItemStore. It would be better to have a test double for ToDoItemStore we could use in the tests for ToDoItemsListViewController.

Follow these steps to add a test double for ToDoItemStore:

1. The first step in implementing a test double for ToDoItemStore is to create a protocol that defines the interface our view controller expects. Add the following protocol to ToDoItemStore.swift:

    ```
    // ToDoItemStore.swift
    protocol ToDoItemStoreProtocol {
      var itemPublisher:
        CurrentValueSubject<[ToDoItem], Never>
          { get set }
      func check(_: ToDoItem)
    }
    ```

    The protocol defines the elements the view controller needs. It needs to subscribe to changes of the items and it also needs a way to check a to-do item.

2. Now that we have the protocol, we can add the conformance to the protocol to ToDoItemStore:

    ```
    // ToDoItemStore.swift
    class ToDoItemStore: ToDoItemStoreProtocol {
      // …
    }
    ```

3. Next, we need a test double conforming to that protocol. Select the **ToDoTests** group in the Project navigator and add a new Swift file with the name `ToDoItemStoreProtocolMock`. Replace the contents of that file with this code:

```swift
// ToDoItemStoreProtocolMock.swift
import Foundation
import Combine
@testable import ToDo

class ToDoItemStoreProtocolMock: ToDoItemStoreProtocol {
  var itemPublisher =
    CurrentValueSubject<[ToDoItem], Never>([])

  var checkLastCallArgument: ToDoItem?
  func check(_ item: ToDoItem) {
    checkLastCallArgument = item
  }
}
```

With this implementation of the test double, we can control how the store used in the view controller behaves. We will see next how we can use this test double in a test.

Using test doubles to implement a number of rows

A table view data source needs to provide two kinds of information: first, the number of rows in a given section and second, the cell for a given item. Sure, there are other methods defined in the `UITableViewDataSource` protocol, but those are optional.

Let's start with the number of rows in a given section. In the default case, the number of sections in a table view is one. This means we are interested in the number of rows in the first and only section. Follow these steps to implement the correct number of rows for the table view:

1. Add the following property to `ToDoItemsListViewControllerTests`:

```swift
// ToDoItemsListViewControllerTests.swift
var toDoItemStoreMock: ToDoItemStoreProtocolMock!
```

2. Next, set it up in `setUpWithError()` and make the system under test use it:

```
// ToDoItemsListViewControllerTests.swift
override func setUpWithError() throws {
  let storyboard = UIStoryboard(name: "Main", bundle:
nil)
  sut = try XCTUnwrap(
    storyboard.instantiateInitialViewController()
    as? ToDoItemsListViewController
  )
  toDoItemStoreMock = ToDoItemStoreProtocolMock()
  sut.toDoItemStore = toDoItemStoreMock
  sut.loadViewIfNeeded()
}
```

This code does not compile because `toDoItemStore` is missing in `ToDoItemsListViewController`.

3. Open `ToDoItemsListViewController` in the editor and add the missing property:

```
// ToDoItemsListViewController.swift
class ToDoItemsListViewController: UIViewController {

  @IBOutlet weak var tableView: UITableView!
  var toDoItemStore: ToDoItemStoreProtocol?
}
```

4. Next, add the following test to `ToDoItemsListViewControllerTests`:

```
// ToDoItemsListViewControllerTests.swift
func test_numberOfRows_whenOneItemIsSent_
shouldReturnOne() {
  toDoItemStoreMock.itemPublisher
    .send([ToDoItem(title: "dummy 1")])

  let result = sut.tableView.numberOfRows(inSection: 0)

  XCTAssertEqual(result, 1)
}
```

In this test, we send a `ToDoItem` instance using its `itemPublisher`. We expect that the table view should then have one row in section zero.

Run all the tests to confirm that this new test fails.

5. At the moment, the table view has no data source set. The `dataSource` property is nil. To make this test pass, we first need to assign `ToDoItemsListViewController` to the `dataSource` property of the table view. Add the following method to `ToDoItemsListViewController`:

```
// ToDoItemsListViewController.swift
override func viewDidLoad() {
  super.viewDidLoad()

  tableView.dataSource = self
}
```

Xcode complains that it **Cannot assign value of type 'ToDoItemsListViewController' to type 'UITableViewDataSource'**. That is expected because `ToDoItemsListViewController` does not yet conform to the `UITableViewDataSource` protocol.

6. Add the following extension to `ToDoItemsListViewController.swift`:

```
// ToDoItemsListViewController.swift
extension ToDoItemsListViewController:
  UITableViewDataSource {

  func tableView(
    _ tableView: UITableView,
    numberOfRowsInSection section: Int) -> Int {

      return 1
    }

  func tableView(
    _ tableView: UITableView,
    cellForRowAt indexPath: IndexPath) -> UITableViewCell
  {

      return UITableViewCell()
```

```
    }
  }
```

This is the minimal code to make `ToDoItemsListViewController` conform to the `UITableViewDataSource` protocol and make the test pass.

You might be wondering why we return a hardcoded fixed value from `tableView(_:numberOfRowsInSection:)`. This is clearly wrong and won't result in a working app. Patience. At the moment, our task is to make the test pass and this is what we have accomplished. Our feeling that this implementation is wrong just means we need another test to make sure the implementation is correct.

7. Add the following test method to `ToDoItemsListViewControllerTests`:

```
// ToDoItemsListViewControllerTests.swift
func test_numberOfRows_whenTwoItemsAreSent_
shouldReturnTwo()
{
  toDoItemStoreMock.itemPublisher
    .send([
      ToDoItem(title: "dummy 1"),
      ToDoItem(title: "dummy 2")
    ])

  let result = sut.tableView.numberOfRows(inSection: 0)

  XCTAssertEqual(result, 2)
}
```

To make this test pass without breaking any previous tests, we need to process the items that are sent by the item publisher in the view controller.

8. First, import Combine and add two properties, `items` and `token`, to `ToDoItemsListViewController`:

```
// ToDoItemsListViewController.swift
class ToDoItemsListViewController: UIViewController {

  @IBOutlet weak var tableView: UITableView!
  var toDoItemStore: ToDoItemStoreProtocol?
  private var items: [ToDoItem] = []
```

```
private var token: AnyCancellable?

    // ...
}
```

The `items` property will hold the items sent by the item publisher and the `token` property will hold a reference to the subscriber subscribed to that publisher. Without a reference to the subscriber, `Combine` would destroy the subscriber before we can use it.

9. Next, change `viewDidLoad()` in `ToDoItemsListViewController` so that it looks like this:

```
// ToDoItemsListViewController.swift
override func viewDidLoad() {
  super.viewDidLoad()

  tableView.dataSource = self
  token = toDoItemStore?.itemPublisher
    .sink(receiveValue: { [weak self] items in

      self?.items = items
  })
}
```

With this code, we subscribe to changes sent by the item publisher of `toDoItemStore`. We store the sent items in the `items` property we just added.

10. Finally, we can return the number of items in `tableView(_:numberOfRowsInSection:)`:

```
// ToDoItemsListViewController.swift
func tableView(
  _ tableView: UITableView,
  numberOfRowsInSection section: Int) -> Int {

    return items.count
}
```

Run the tests. All the tests pass.

Next, we are going to use our test double to implement the to-do item cell for the table view.

Using test doubles to implement setting up the to-do item cell

As always, when implementing a new microfeature, we need a test. Follow these steps to add the failing test and the implementation that makes the test pass:

1. Add the following test method to `ToDoItemsListViewControllerTests.swift`:

```
// ToDoItemsListViewControllerTests.swift
func test_cellForRowAt_shouldReturnCellWithTitle() throws
{
    let titleUnderTest = "dummy 1"
    toDoItemStoreMock.itemPublisher
        .send([ToDoItem(title: titleUnderTest)])
    let tableView = try XCTUnwrap(sut.tableView)

    let indexPath = IndexPath(row: 0, section: 0)
    let cell = try XCTUnwrap(
        tableView.dataSource?
            .tableView(tableView,
                       cellForRowAt: indexPath)
        as? ToDoItemCell
    )


}
```

This is not the complete test, but we need to pause here because the `ToDoItemCell` type is not yet defined.

2. Select the **ToDo** group in the Project navigator and add a new **Cocoa Touch** class via the **File** menu. In the **Class** field, insert the name `ToDoItemCell` and make it a **Subclass of** `UITableViewCell`. Remove the template code within the class.

3. Go back to `ToDoItemsListViewControllerTests` and add the test assertion, as shown in the following code block:

```swift
// ToDoItemsListViewControllerTests.swift
func test_cellForRowAt_shouldReturnCellWithTitle1()
throws {
  let titleUnderTest = "dummy 1"
  toDoItemStoreMock.itemPublisher
    .send([ToDoItem(title: titleUnderTest)])
  let tableView = try XCTUnwrap(sut.tableView)

  let indexPath = IndexPath(row: 0, section: 0)
  let cell = try XCTUnwrap(
    tableView.dataSource?
      .tableView(tableView,
                 cellForRowAt: indexPath)
    as? ToDoItemCell
  )

  XCTAssertEqual(cell.titleLabel.text, titleUnderTest)
}
```

In this test, we publish a list with one to-do item using our test double. Then we execute the `tableView(_:cellForRowAt:)` method defined in the data source of the table view. The returned table view cell should have a label showing the title of the to-do item sent by the publisher. This test does not compile at the moment because the cell doesn't have a property with the name `titleLabel`.

4. Add the property to `ToDoItemCell`:

```swift
// ToDoItemCell.swift
class ToDoItemCell: UITableViewCell {
  let titleLabel = UILabel()
}
```

Now the tests compile. Run the tests to confirm that the new test fails.

If you are an experienced iOS developer, you might have realized that this code is not enough. The label is initialized, but it is not added to the cell. We will fix that later in this section.

5. The test we have just added fails because the data source of the table view does not return a cell of the `ToDoItemCell` type. Go to `ToDoItemsListViewController` and replace the `tableView(_:cellForRowAt:)` method with the following code:

```
// ToDoItemsListViewController.swift
func tableView(
    _ tableView: UITableView,
    cellForRowAt indexPath: IndexPath) -> UITableViewCell {
        let cell = ToDoItemCell()
        cell.titleLabel.text = "dummy 1"
        return cell
}
```

Even though this code makes all the tests pass (run the tests to confirm), these few lines of code have several issues. One issue is that the text in `titleLabel` is hardcoded to the string expected by the test. It might seem stupid to write code like this, but this is kind of essential to TDD. Code that uses hardcoded values to make the tests pass tells us that we need more tests.

6. Add the following test to `ToDoItemsListViewController`:

```
// ToDoItemsListViewControllerTests.swift
func test_cellForRowAt_shouldReturnCellWithTitle2()
throws
{
    let titleUnderTest = "dummy 2"
    toDoItemStoreMock.itemPublisher
        .send([
            ToDoItem(title: "dummy 1"),
            ToDoItem(title: titleUnderTest)
        ])
    let tableView = try XCTUnwrap(sut.tableView)

    let indexPath = IndexPath(row: 1, section: 0)
    let cell = try XCTUnwrap(
        tableView.dataSource?
            .tableView(tableView,
                       cellForRowAt: indexPath)
```

```
        as? ToDoItemCell
    )

    XCTAssertEqual(cell.titleLabel.text, titleUnderTest)
}
```

You should try to find a better name for this test. I use this name here to keep the method name kind of short. Long method names do not look good in printed books.

In this test, we send two to-do items to the system under test and check the text in the second cell. Run the tests. This new test fails because the text in `titleLabel` is hardcoded.

7. Change the implementation of `tableView(_:cellForRowAt:)` such that it looks like this:

```
// ToDoItemsListViewController.swift
func tableView(
    _ tableView: UITableView,
    cellForRowAt indexPath: IndexPath) -> UITableViewCell {

    let cell = ToDoItemCell()

    let item = items[indexPath.row]
    cell.titleLabel.text = item.title

    return cell
}
```

In this code, we get the item for that row from the `items` property and assign its title to the text of the `titleLabel` property. Run the tests to confirm that all the tests pass.

The implementation code still has an issue. The cells in a table view should be reused to improve the rendering performance of the table view. Let's refactor the code without breaking the tests.

8. To opt in to the cell reuse capability of `UITableView`, add the following lines of code to `viewDidLoad()` in `ToDoItemsListViewController`:

```
// ToDoItemsListViewController.swift
tableView.register(
```

```
    ToDoItemCell.self,
    forCellReuseIdentifier: "ToDoItemCell"
)
```

With this call, we register `ToDoItemCell` for the reuse queue of the table view.

9. Now we can ask the table view to dequeue such a cell in
    `tableView(_:cellForRowAt:)`:

```swift
// ToDoItemsListViewController.swift
func tableView(
    _ tableView: UITableView,
    cellForRowAt indexPath: IndexPath) -> UITableViewCell {

    let cell = tableView.dequeueReusableCell(
        withIdentifier: "ToDoItemCell",
        for: indexPath
    ) as! ToDoItemCell

    let item = items[indexPath.row]
    cell.titleLabel.text = item.title

    return cell
}
```

Run the tests to confirm that we didn't break anything.

The implementation of `ToDoItemCell` is not enough to make the cell show the title in the user interface. We have initialized the label, but we haven't added it to any view yet. This is what we will do next.

We could write tests that check whether the label is added to the table view cell in the tests for the view controller. But if we think about it, they belong to dedicated tests for the cell itself. Follow these steps to add the test and the implementation that make the test pass:

1. Select the **ToDoTests** group in the Project navigation and add a new **Unit Test Case Class** file from the **File** menu. Insert the name `ToDoItemCellTests` in the **Text** field next to **Class** and create the file. Remove the two template tests in the created file.

2. Below the existing import statement, add the testable import of the ToDo module:

```
// ToDoItemCellTests.swift
import XCTest
@testable import ToDo
```

3. Before we can test anything relating to the table view cell, we need to set it up. Replace the implementation of the ToDoItemCellTests class with the following code:

```
// ToDoItemCellTests.swift
class ToDoItemCellTests: XCTestCase {

    var sut: ToDoItemCell!

    override func setUpWithError() throws {
        sut = ToDoItemCell()
    }

    override func tearDownWithError() throws {
        sut = nil
    }
}
```

4. Now we are ready to add the first test to this new test class. Add the following test method:

```
// ToDoItemCellTests.swift
func test_hasTitleLabelSubview() {
    let subview = sut.titleLabel
    XCTAssertTrue(subview.isDescendant(of: sut.
contentView))
}
```

The isDescendant(of:) method is defined on UIView. We have already seen this call earlier in this chapter when we wrote a test that asserted that the table view was added to the view of the view controller.

Run the tests to confirm that this new test fails.

5. To make this test pass, change the code in `ToDoItemCell` such that it looks like this:

```swift
// ToDoItemCell.swift
class ToDoItemCell: UITableViewCell {

    let titleLabel = UILabel()

    override init(style: UITableViewCell.CellStyle,
                  reuseIdentifier: String?) {

        super.init(style: style,
                   reuseIdentifier: reuseIdentifier)

        contentView.addSubview(titleLabel)
    }

    required init?(coder: NSCoder) { fatalError() }
}
```

Run the tests to confirm that this code makes the test pass.

6. Now that the test passes, we move to the refactoring stage of the TDD workflow. Depending on your style of development, you may already be satisfied with this implementation. I like to structure the initialization of user interface elements differently. I would refactor that code to this:

```swift
// ToDoItemCell.swift
class ToDoItemCell: UITableViewCell {

    let titleLabel: UILabel

    override init(style: UITableViewCell.CellStyle,
                  reuseIdentifier: String?) {

        titleLabel = UILabel()
```

```
        super.init(style: style,
                    reuseIdentifier: reuseIdentifier)

        contentView.addSubview(titleLabel)
    }

    required init?(coder: NSCoder) { fatalError() }
}
```

The difference is that I prefer to initialize the elements within the `init` method. Run the test to confirm that all the tests still pass.

Note that we have intentionally not implemented any positioning of the label. In my opinion, this is something we shouldn't test with a unit test. The positioning and the size of user interface elements depend on the size of the screen and the version of iOS. We could write tests for these values, but most probably, those would often break even though the app still works for the user. With our tests, we want to catch the real bugs.

OK, this test was easy. Let's now add the two other required labels – `dateLabel` and `locationLabel`:

1. Add this test method to `ToDoItemCellTests`:

    ```
    // ToDoItemCellTests.swift
    func test_hasDateLabelSubview() {
        let subview = sut.dateLabel
        XCTAssertTrue(subview.isDescendant(of: sut.
    contentView))
    }
    ```

2. Run the tests to confirm that this new test fails. The test fails because the `dateLabel` property is missing.

3. Go to `ToDoItemCell` and add this property:

    ```
    // ToDoItemCell.swift
    class ToDoItemCell: UITableViewCell {

        let titleLabel: UILabel
        let dateLabel: UILabel

        override init(style: UITableViewCell.CellStyle,
    ```

```
                  reuseIdentifier: String?) {

      titleLabel = UILabel()
      dateLabel = UILabel()

      super.init(style: style,
                 reuseIdentifier: reuseIdentifier)

      contentView.addSubview(titleLabel)
   }

   required init?(coder: NSCoder) { fatalError() }
}
```

"Wait a minute, Dominik," I hear you say, "why didn't you add the label to the content view?" Good question! In TDD, you should only add code that makes the test pass. The test failed because the label was not defined. So, our task in this step is to add this `dateLabel` property. At the moment, we don't know whether this is enough to make the test pass. We have the feeling that this is not enough based on our previous experience with `titleLabel`, but it's better to confirm our feeling.

Run the tests to confirm that the test is still failing. It still fails, but this time in the line of the assert function call.

4. To make it pass, add the following line below the existing `addSubview` call:

```
// ToDoItemCell.swift
contentView.addSubview(dateLabel)
```

Run the tests again. Now, all the tests pass again.

5. When the `location` property of the to-do item is set, the cell should show the name of the `location` property. Add the following test to `ToDoItemCellTests`:

```
// ToDoItemCellTests.swift
func test_hasLocationLabelSubview() {
   let subview = sut.locationLabel
   XCTAssertTrue(subview.isDescendant(of: sut.
   contentView))
}
```

Run the tests to see this test failing.

6. Add the property for the location label to ToDoItemCell:

```swift
// ToDoItemCell.swift

class ToDoItemCell: UITableViewCell {

    let titleLabel: UILabel
    let dateLabel: UILabel
    let locationLabel: UILabel

    override init(style: UITableViewCell.CellStyle,
                  reuseIdentifier: String?) {

        titleLabel = UILabel()
        dateLabel = UILabel()
        locationLabel = UILabel()

        super.init(style: style,
                   reuseIdentifier: reuseIdentifier)

        contentView.addSubview(titleLabel)
        contentView.addSubview(dateLabel)
    }

    required init?(coder: NSCoder) { fatalError() }
}
```

Run the tests to see the last test still failing, but now in the line with the assert function call.

7. Add the line that adds locationLabel as a subview to contentView of the cell:

```swift
// ToDoItemCell.swift:
contentView.addSubview(locationLabel)
```

Run all the tests to make sure they all pass now.

The next step is to fill the labels in the data source of the table view. Open `ToDoItemsListViewControllerTests` and follow these steps to add this feature to our app:

1. Add the following test to `ToDoItemsListViewControllerTests`:

```
// ToDoItemsListViewControllerTests.swift
func test_cellForRowAt_shouldReturnCellWithDate() throws
{
  let date = Date()
  toDoItemStoreMock.itemPublisher
    .send([
      ToDoItem(title: "dummy 1",
               timestamp: date.timeIntervalSince1970)
    ])
  let tableView = try XCTUnwrap(sut.tableView)

  let indexPath = IndexPath(row: 0, section: 0)
  let cell = try XCTUnwrap(
    tableView.dataSource?
      .tableView(tableView,
                 cellForRowAt: indexPath)
    as? ToDoItemCell
  )

  XCTAssertEqual(cell.dateLabel.text,
                 sut.dateFormatter.string(from: date))
}
```

Here, we now use `toDoItemStoreMock` to send a to-do item with a timestamp. In the `assert` function, we use a `dateFormatter` property that is not defined yet. Let's add this property to make the test compile.

2. Go to `ToDoItemsListViewController` and add the following property:

```
// ToDoItemsListViewController.swift
let dateFormatter = DateFormatter()
```

Now the test compiles. Run the tests to confirm that this new test fails.

3. To make the test pass, we need to set the date label in
    `tableView(_:cellForRowAt:)`. Add the following code right below `cell.`
    `textLabel.text = item.title`:

```
// ToDoItemsListViewController.swift
if let timestamp = item.timestamp {
    let date = Date(timeIntervalSince1970: timestamp)
    cell.dateLabel.text = dateFormatter.string(from: date)
}
```

We use the timestamp of the item to generate a date from it and ask the date
formatter for a string representation of that date.

Run all the tests to confirm that all the tests pass.

The next step is to refactor the implementation. We could move the generation of the date
string to the model object, but then the model object would need to know how the data
is presented to the user. This is not a good idea. It would be better to move that code to a
view model. That is a class connected to the view controller that converts the model data
such that it can be presented in the user interface.

We will leave it as it is because for our small app, it's OK to have this code in the
view controller.

You will implement the setting of the `location` label in the exercises later in this chapter.

We have now implemented the presentation and the setup of the to-do item table view
cells. With the tests in place, we can now look at the implementation and see whether we
can improve it to better fit modern concepts in iOS development. The implementation we
have built here is based on how table views have been implemented for many years. Over
the last few years, better ways have emerged to set up a table view.

In the following section, we will refactor our implementation to use a diffable data source.

Refactoring to a diffable data source

In iOS 13, Apple introduced the `UITableViewDiffableDataSource` class. This
class manages the update of a table view when the data changes and it can be used as the
data source of any table view. It should be used, when possible, because implementing
updates of a table view is a bit complicated and can lead to strange bugs and even crashes.
In addition, the code needed to set up such a data source is often easier to read and reason
about than the traditional implementation we used in the previous section.

Follow these steps to transform our implementation to one that uses a diffable data source:

1. A diffable data source manages the data in the table view using a section and an item that both need to conform to the `Hashable` protocol. We already have an item we can use in the diffable data source, the `ToDoItem` structure. However, this structure does not yet conform to `Hashable`. To make it conform to that protocol, add the following code to `ToDoItem.swift` outside of the current `ToDoItem` implementation:

```swift
// ToDoItem.swift
extension ToDoItem: Hashable {
  func hash(into hasher: inout Hasher) {
    hasher.combine(id)
  }
}
```

    With this code, we tell the hasher provided by Swift to use the ID of the to-do item to generate the hash value. The ID of the to-do item is unique and therefore a good basis for a hash value.

2. Next, we need a section type that also conforms to `Hashable`. Add the following enum type to `ToDoItemsListViewController.swift`:

```swift
// ToDoItemsListViewController.swift
enum Section {
  case main
}
```

    This is enough for now. We only need one section at the moment because later we will add another section to distinguish between to-do and done items.

3. Next, we need a property for the data source. Add the following property to `ToDoItemsListViewController`:

```swift
// ToDoItemsListViewController.swift
private var dataSource:
  UITableViewDiffableDataSource<Section, ToDoItem>?
```

4. In the `viewDidLoad()` method, replace the `tableView.dataSource = self` code with the following:

```swift
// ToDoItemsListViewController.swift
dataSource =
```

```swift
UITableViewDiffableDataSource<Section, ToDoItem>(
  tableView: tableView,
  cellProvider: { [weak self] tableView, indexPath, item
  in

    let cell = tableView.dequeueReusableCell(
      withIdentifier: "ToDoItemCell",
      for: indexPath
    ) as! ToDoItemCell

    cell.titleLabel.text = item.title
    if let timestamp = item.timestamp {
      let date = Date(timeIntervalSince1970: timestamp)
      cell.dateLabel.text = self?.dateFormatter
        .string(from: date)
    }

    return cell
})
```

With this code, we initialize a diffable data source for the table view. The second parameter of this initializer is a `cell` provider. This piece of code gets called when the table view needs to show a `cell` provider for a given index path. As you can see, the code within this closure looks similar to the code we had in `tableView(_:cellForRowAt:)` previously.

5. Now delete the extension that implemented the conformance to `UITableViewDataSource` within `ToDoItemsListViewController.swift`.

6. `UITableViewDiffableDataSource` manages table view updates via `NSDiffableDataSourceSnapshot`. To update the table view with new data, we need to create a snapshot and set it up with the new data. Add the following method to `ToDoItemsListViewController`:

```swift
// ToDoItemsListViewController.swift
private func update(with items: [ToDoItem]) {
  var snapshot =
  NSDiffableDataSourceSnapshot<Section, ToDoItem>()
  snapshot.appendSections([.main])
```

```
    snapshot.appendItems(items)
    dataSource?.apply(snapshot)
}
```

In this method, we create a snapshot and add one section and the items passed into that method.

7. The view controller receives updates from the publisher of `toDoItemStore`. Change the subscription code in `viewDidLoad` such that it looks like this:

```
// ToDoItemsListViewController.swift
token = toDoItemStore?.itemPublisher
    .sink(receiveValue: { [weak self] items in
        self?.items = items
        self?.update(with: items)
    })
```

In addition to assigning the received items to the `items` property of the view controller, we call here the new update method that applies a new snapshot to the data source.

Run the tests. All the tests pass. We have now successfully refactored our table view code to use a diffable data source.

Our list of to-do items should show two sections, one for the to-do items and one for the already done items. In the next section, we will change the snapshot creation to achieve this.

Presenting two sections

As we have already refactored to a diffable data source, supporting two sections in the table view is quite easy. Follow these steps to implement two sections:

1. As always, we need to start with a failing test. Add the following test to `ToDoItemsListViewControllerTests`:

```
// ToDoItemsListViewControllerTests.swift
func test_numberOfSections_shouldReturnTwo() {
    var doneItem = ToDoItem(title: "dummy 2")
    doneItem.done = true
    toDoItemStoreMock.itemPublisher
        .send([ToDoItem(title: "dummy 1"),
```

```
                doneItem])

  let result = sut.tableView.numberOfSections

  XCTAssertEqual(result, 2)
}
```

In this test, we set a to-do item and a done item to the table view using `toDoItemStoreMock`. The name of the test method should also include what the preconditions of the tests are. We use a shorter name in the book because otherwise, the code is harder to read. You should try to use a better name.

Run the tests to confirm that this new test fails.

2. To support two sections, enum `Section` needs two cases. Change the code of enum `Section` such that it looks like this:

```
// ToDoItemsListViewController.swift
enum Section {
  case todo
  case done
}
```

3. Finally, we need to change the `update` method such that it looks like this:

```
// ToDoItemsListViewController.swift
private func update(with items: [ToDoItem]) {
  var snapshot =
  NSDiffableDataSourceSnapshot<Section, ToDoItem>()
  snapshot.appendSections([.todo, .done])
  snapshot.appendItems(
    items.filter({ false == $0.done }),
    toSection: .todo)
  snapshot.appendItems(
    items.filter({ $0.done }),
    toSection: .done)
  dataSource?.apply(snapshot)
}
```

In this code, we add the two sections to the snapshot and use the done property of the to-do item to fill the two sections.

Run the tests to confirm that this code makes the new test pass.

The data source of the table view is now finished. The next step in implementing the list view of the to-do items is to add code that reacts to the user selecting the to-do item in the list.

Implementing the delegate of a table view

When the user selects a to-do item in the list of items, the details of the to-do item should be shown in a dedicated view. We will implement the actual navigation between the different views of the app in *Chapter 11, Easy Navigation with Coordinators*. In this section, we will implement the required code in ToDoItemsListViewController.

Follow these steps to prepare ToDoItemsListViewController for navigation to the detail view:

1. Let's assume we already have a delegate that will provide a method the view controller can call. Add the following test method to ToDoItemsListViewControllerTests:

    ```
    // ToDoItemsListViewControllerTests.swift
    func test_didSelectCellAt_shouldCallDelegate() throws {
      let delegateMock =
        ToDoItemsListViewControllerProtocolMock()
    }
    ```

    Xcode tells us that it cannot find the ToDoItemsListViewControllerProtocolMock type. This type is meant to be a mock object for the real delegate we will add in *Chapter 11, Easy Navigation with Coordinators*. The view controller should tell the delegate that a to-do item was selected by the user. Let's add a mock object with a method for that task.

2. Select the **ToDoTests** group in the Project navigator and add a new Swift file. Insert the name `ToDoItemsListViewControllerProtocolMock` in the **Save As** field and then click **Create**. Replace the contents of the created file with the following:

```swift
// ToDoItemsListViewControllerProtocolMock.swift
import UIKit
@testable import ToDo

class ToDoItemsListViewControllerProtocolMock:
  ToDoItemsListViewControllerProtocol {
}
```

Again, Xcode tells us that a type is missing. This time, Xcode doesn't know anything about `ToDoItemsListViewControllerProtocol`.

3. Go to `ToDoItemsListViewController.swift` and add the following protocol below the import statements:

```swift
// ToDoItemsListViewController.swift
protocol ToDoItemsListViewControllerProtocol {
  func selectToDoItem(
    _ viewController: UIViewController,
    item: ToDoItem)
}
```

4. Now we can finish the implementation of the protocol mock:

```swift
// ToDoItemsListViewControllerProtocolMock.swift
class ToDoItemsListViewControllerProtocolMock:
  ToDoItemsListViewControllerProtocol {

  var selectToDoItemReceivedArguments:
  (viewController: UIViewController,
   item: ToDoItem)?

  func selectToDoItem(
    _ viewController: UIViewController,
    item: ToDoItem) {
```

```
        selectToDoItemReceivedArguments =
          (viewController, item)
    }
  }
```

This protocol mock stores the received argument to the call of the delegate method, selectToDoItem(_:item:).

5. Now that we have this protocol mock, we can use it in our test:

```
// ToDoItemsListViewControllerTest.swift
func test_didSelectCellAt_shouldCallDelegate() throws {
  let delegateMock =
    ToDoItemsListViewControllerProtocolMock()
  sut.delegate = delegateMock
}
```

We have to stop here because sut doesn't yet have a delegate property.

6. Add that property to ToDoItemsListViewController:

```
// ToDoItemsListViewController.swift
var delegate: ToDoItemsListViewControllerProtocol?
```

7. Now we can finish the test method:

```
// ToDoItemsListViewControllerTests.swift
func test_didSelectCellAt_shouldCallDelegate() throws {
  let delegateMock =
    ToDoItemsListViewControllerProtocolMock()
  sut.delegate = delegateMock
  let toDoItem = ToDoItem(title: "dummy 1")
  toDoItemStoreMock.itemPublisher
    .send([toDoItem])
  let tableView = try XCTUnwrap(sut.tableView)

  let indexPath = IndexPath(row: 0, section: 0)
  tableView.delegate?.tableView?(
    tableView,
    didSelectRowAt: indexPath)
```

```
XCTAssertEqual(
    delegateMock.selectToDoItemReceivedArguments?.item,
    toDoItem)
}
```

After we have set the delegate of the system under test, we send one to-do item using `itemPublisher` of `toDoItemStoreMock`. Next, we call `tableView(_:didSelectRowAt:)` of the `tableViews` delegate. Finally, we assert that the protocol method, `selectToDoItem(_:item:)`, got called with the selected to-do item.

Run the tests to confirm that this new test fails.

8. To make the test pass, add the follow extension to `ToDoItemsListViewController.swift` outside of the class definition of `ToDoItemsListViewController`:

```swift
// ToDoItemsListViewController.swift
extension ToDoItemsListViewController:
    UITableViewDelegate {

    func tableView(_ tableView: UITableView,
                   didSelectRowAt indexPath: IndexPath) {

        let item = items[indexPath.row]
        delegate?.selectToDoItem(self, item: item)
    }
}
```

In this implementation, we get the to-do item of the selected cell and call the delegate method with it.

9. To make `ToDoItemsListViewController` the delegate of the table view, add the following line to the end of `viewDidLoad()`:

```swift
// ToDoItemsListViewController.swift
tableView.delegate = self
```

Now, run the tests to confirm that all the tests pass.

For now, we are finished with implementing the list view of the to-do items.

Summary

In this chapter, we have learned how to test table views and table view cells. We experienced the value of useful unit tests when refactoring a large part of the code. By switching from the traditional table view data source to the diffable data source, we improved the code and the behavior of the app while still keeping the existing tested functionality.

In the next chapter, we will use the knowledge we gained to create a detailed view and its view controller.

Exercises

1. Implement the setting of the location label using test-driven development.
2. Try to figure out in the documentation of Xcode how to add section headers when using a diffable data source. We will implement the section headers in *Chapter 11, Easy Navigation with Coordinators*.

8
Building a Simple Detail View

Often in iOS development, table views or collection views just give a brief summary of the presented items. To figure out all the details of the shown items, the user has to select an item so that they can be redirected to the details. In the details view, the user can often interact with the shown item.

For example, in a mail app, the summary only shows the sender, the subject, and the first few lines of the mail. To read the complete mail and to answer it, the user has to open it in the details view.

In this chapter, we will build the details view for our to-do items. The chapter is structured as follows:

- Adding labels, a button, and a map
- Filling in the data
- Checking the to-do item

We start by adding the user interface elements to the view.

Technical requirements

The source code for this chapter is available here:

https://github.com/PacktPublishing/Test-Driven-iOS-
Development-with-Swift-Fourth-Edition/tree/main/chapter08

Adding labels, a button, and a map

We have done this so often already that you might guess what we have to do first. That's right, we need a test case class for our tests. Select the **ToDoTests** group in the project navigator in Xcode and add a new **Unit Test Case Class** called ToDoItemDetailsViewControllerTests. Make sure that it is added to the unit test target:

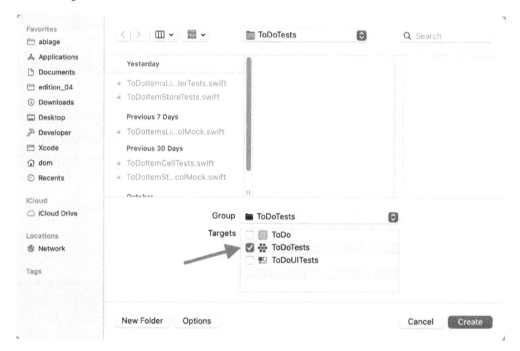

Figure 8.1 – The test case needs to be added to the unit test target

Remove the two template tests in the created test case class and add @testable import ToDo below the existing import statement:

```
// ToDoItemDetailsViewControllerTests.swift
import XCTest
@testable import ToDo
```

```
class ToDoItemDetailsViewControllerTests: XCTestCase {
  override func setUpWithError() throws {
  }
  override func tearDownWithError() throws {
  }
}
```

The details view needs some labels to show the information of the to-do item. Let's start with the label for the title. Follow these steps:

1. Add the following property for the system under test:

    ```
    // ToDoItemDetailsViewControllerTests.swift
    var sut: ToDoItemDetailsViewController!
    ```

    Xcode complains that it **Cannot find type 'ToDoItemDetailsViewController' in scope**.

2. Select the **ToDo** group in the project navigator and add a new Cocoa Touch **Class** with the name `ToDoItemDetailsViewController`. Make it a subclass of **UIViewController**:

Figure 8.2 – Options for the view controller class

3. Remove the template code inside the created class. Go back to
    `ToDoItemDetailsViewControllerTests`. Xcode should remove the error
    after a few seconds. If it doesn't, select the **Product | Build** menu item to compile
    the project.

4. Now we have two choices. One, we could build the user interface in code as we
    did for the table view cells in the previous chapter. Two, we could use a storyboard
    for the user interface. To give you a broader picture in this book, we will use the
    storyboard for the user interface in this chapter.

    Replace the `setUpWithError()` and the `tearDownWithError()` methods
    with the following implementation:

    ```swift
    // ToDoItemDetailsViewControllerTests.swift
    override func setUpWithError() throws {
        let storyboard = UIStoryboard(name: "Main", bundle:
          nil)
        sut = (storyboard.instantiateViewController(
          withIdentifier: "ToDoItemDetailsViewController")
          as! ToDoItemDetailsViewController)
        sut.loadViewIfNeeded()
    }
    override func tearDownWithError() throws {
        sut = nil
    }
    ```

    The parentheses around `(storyboard.`
    `instantiateViewController(withIdentifier:`
    `"ToDoItemDetailsViewController") as!`
    `ToDoItemDetailsViewController)` are needed to silence a warning
    produced by Xcode. Try and see what Xcode tells you do when you omit them.

5. With the setup and the teardown methods in place, we can write the first test of that
    test case class:

    ```swift
    // ToDoItemDetailsViewControllerTests.swift
    func test_view_shouldHaveTitleLabel() throws {
        let subview = try XCTUnwrap(sut.titleLabel)
    }
    ```

This test is not finished yet but we have to pause here because the `titleLabel` property is missing.

6. Add the property to `ToDoItemDetailsViewController`:

```
// ToDoItemDetailsViewController.swift
class ToDoItemDetailsViewController: UIViewController {
    @IBOutlet var titleLabel: UILabel!
}
```

7. Now we can finish the test method:

```
// ToDoItemDetailsViewControllerTests.swift
func test_view_shouldHaveTitleLabel() throws {
    let subview = try XCTUnwrap(sut.titleLabel)
    XCTAssertTrue(subview.isDescendant(of: sut.view))
}
```

8. Run all tests to confirm that this new test fails. This test fails in `setUpWithError()`. Click the red diamond in the failure message to see what the problem is:

```
12    override func setUpWithError() throws {
13        let storyboard = UIStoryboard(name: "Main",
              bundle: nil)
14        sut = (storyboard.instantiateViewController(
15            withId   ◈  Storyboard (<UIStoryboard:         ⊗
                "T      0x6000034b8420>) doesn't contain a view
                        controller with identifier
16                      'ToDoItemDetailsViewController' (NSInvalidAr
17        sut.loa      gumentException)
18    }
19
```

Figure 8.3 – The storyboard doesn't have a view controller with the identifier 'ToDoItemDetailsViewController'

Looking at the problem shown in *Figure 8.3*, we need to add a new scene for that view controller to the storyboard.

9. Open the `Main.storyboard` file in the Interface Builder in Xcode and click the plus (+) button in the toolbar:

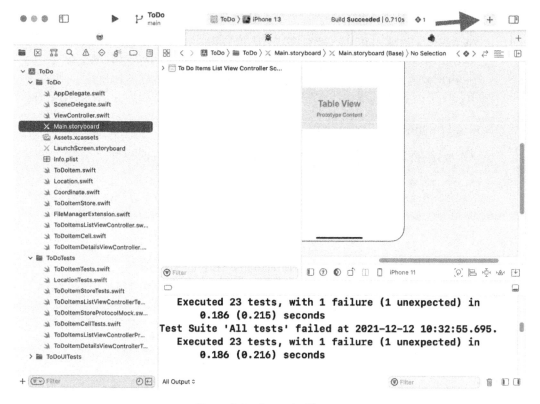

Figure 8.4 – Open the library

10. Search for `view controller` and drag a **View Controller** object onto the storyboard. Open the **Identity** inspector by selecting the **View | Inspectors | Identity** menu item. Change **Class** and **Storyboard ID** to **ToDoItemDetailsViewController**:

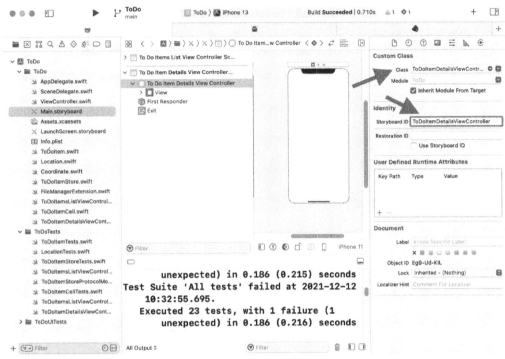

Figure 8.5 – Changing the class and the storyboard ID of the scene

Run the tests again. The new test still fails because the `titleLabel` property is `nil`.

11. We need to add a label to the storyboard scene and connect it with `IBOutlet`. Open the library by selecting the **View | Show Library** menu item. Drag a **Label** object onto the storyboard scene of `ToDoItemDetailsViewController`:

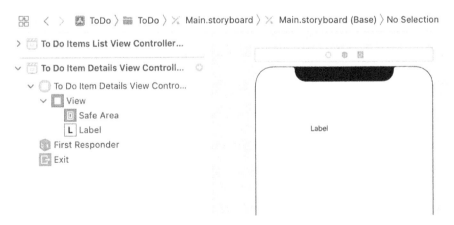

Figure 8.6 – The added label on the To Do Item Details View Controller scene

12. Open the **Assistant** editor by selecting the **Editor | Assistant** menu item. Xcode automatically opens `ToDoItemsDetailsViewController` in the **Assistant** editor. If it opens another file, close Xcode and restart it.

Hold down the *Ctrl* key and drag a connection from the label in the storyboard to the `IBOutlet` property in the code:

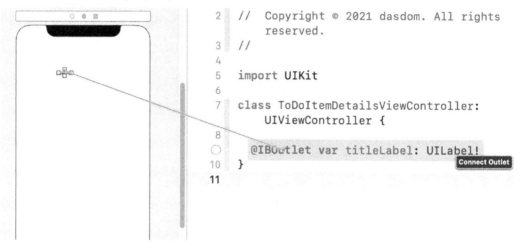

Figure 8.7 – Connect the label in the scene with the IBOutlet property

Run the tests again. All tests pass.

As we have hardly written any code, there is nothing to refactor.

In the same way, you can add the labels for the date, the location, and the description of the to-do item. We won't show this here because it works exactly the same as adding the label for the title. Follow the steps again with a different name for the property. To get you started, here are the three tests for these three new labels:

```
// ToDoItemDetailsViewControllerTests.swift
func test_view_shouldHaveDateLabel() throws {
    let subview = try XCTUnwrap(sut.dateLabel)
    XCTAssertTrue(subview.isDescendant(of: sut.view))
}
func test_view_shouldHaveLocationLabel() throws {
    let subview = try XCTUnwrap(sut.locationLabel)
    XCTAssertTrue(subview.isDescendant(of: sut.view))
}
func test_view_shouldHaveDescriptionLabel() throws {
    let subview = try XCTUnwrap(sut.descriptionLabel)
```

```
XCTAssertTrue(subview.isDescendant(of: sut.view))
}
```

Add these tests one by one and make them pass. But make sure to only have one failing test at any time.

Next, we need a map view to show the location of the to-do item if the location is set. Follow these steps to add it to the view:

1. Add the following test to `ToDoItemDetailsViewControllerTests`:

   ```
   // ToDoItemDetailsViewControllerTests.swift
   func test_view_shouldHaveMapView() throws {
     let subview = try XCTUnwrap(sut.mapView)
     XCTAssertTrue(subview.isDescendant(of: sut.view))
   }
   ```

   Run the test to confirm that this new test fails.

2. Add the `MapKit` import to `ToDoItemDetailsViewController` and add an outlet for the `mapView` view:

   ```
   // ToDoItemDetailsViewController.swift
   import UIKit
   import MapKit

   class ToDoItemDetailsViewController: UIViewController {
     @IBOutlet var titleLabel: UILabel!
     @IBOutlet var dateLabel: UILabel!
     @IBOutlet var locationLabel: UILabel!
     @IBOutlet var descriptionLabel: UILabel!
     @IBOutlet var mapView: MKMapView!
   }
   ```

   Run the test again. It still fails, but this time because the `mapView` property is `nil`.

3. Open `Main.storyboard` and drag a **Map Kit View** onto the **To Do Item Details View Controller** scene. Next, open the Assistant editor and hold down the *Ctrl* key while you drag a connection to the `IBOutlet` property of the map view.

   Run the tests to confirm that all tests now pass.

The last UI element we have to add to the view is the button to mark an item as **Done**. This works the same way as adding the labels previously. So again, this is left as an exercise for you. Here is the test to get you started:

```swift
// ToDoItemDetailsViewControllerTests.swift
func test_view_shouldHaveDoneButton() throws {
    let subview = try XCTUnwrap(sut.doneButton)
    XCTAssertTrue(subview.isDescendant(of: sut.view))
}
```

Make this test pass by adding a `UIButton` instance to the view controller.

Before we move on, you should take some time to make this user interface better. Move the elements and add layout constraints so that the user interface is more pleasing to the eye. When you've finished, your result could look similar to the following figure:

Figure 8.8 – The user interface for the details view

Now that we have the user interface for the details view, we can present the data of the to-do item when the details are pushed onto the screen. This is what we will implement in the following section.

Filling in the data

Follow these steps to update the user interface with the data from the to-do item:

1. We start with a new test. Add the following test method to `ToDoItemDetailsViewControllerTests`:

    ```swift
    // TodoItemDetailsViewControllerTests.swift
    func test_settingToDoItem_shouldUpdateTitleLabel() {
        let title = "dummy title"
        let toDoItem = ToDoItem(title: title)
        sut.toDoItem = toDoItem
    }
    ```

    At this point, we get an error from Xcode that **Value of type 'ToDoItemDetailsViewController' has no member 'toDoItem'**.

2. Go to `ToDoItemDetailsViewController` and add the `toDoItem` property:

    ```swift
    // ToDoItemDetailsViewController.swift
    class ToDoItemDetailsViewController: UIViewController {
        @IBOutlet var titleLabel: UILabel!
        @IBOutlet var dateLabel: UILabel!
        @IBOutlet var locationLabel: UILabel!
        @IBOutlet var descriptionLabel: UILabel!
        @IBOutlet var mapView: MKMapView!
        @IBOutlet var doneButton: UIButton!
        var toDoItem: ToDoItem?
    }
    ```

3. Now we can finish writing the test by adding the `Assert` call:

    ```swift
    // ToDoItemDetailsViewControllerTests.swift
    func test_settingToDoItem_shouldUpdateTitleLabel() {
        let title = "dummy title"
        let toDoItem = ToDoItem(title: title)
        sut.toDoItem = toDoItem
    ```

```
    XCTAssertEqual(sut.titleLabel.text, title)
  }
```

Run the tests to confirm that this new test fails.

4. Go back to the implementation code and replace the property declaration with the following:

```
// ToDoItemDetailsViewController.swift
var toDoItem: ToDoItem? {
  didSet {
    titleLabel.text = toDoItem?.title
  }
}
```

Run the tests again to confirm that all tests now pass.

The tests and the implementation for the other labels work in a similar way, and are left for you to do as an exercise. To get you started, here are the tests:

```
// ToDoItemDetailsViewControllerTests.swift
func test_settingToDoItem_shouldUpdateDateLabel() {
  let date = Date()
  let toDoItem = ToDoItem(
    title: "dummy title",
    timestamp: date.timeIntervalSince1970)

  sut.toDoItem = toDoItem

  XCTAssertEqual(sut.dateLabel.text,
                 sut.dateFormatter.string(from: date))
}
func test_settingToDoItem_shouldUpdateDescriptionLabel() {
  let description = "dummy discription"
  let toDoItem = ToDoItem(
    title: "dummy title",
    itemDescription: description)

  sut.toDoItem = toDoItem
```

```
XCTAssertEqual(sut.descriptionLabel.text, description)
}
func test_settingToDoItem_shouldUpdateLocationLabel() {
  let location = "dummy location"
  let toDoItem = ToDoItem(
    title: "dummy title",
    location: Location(name: location))

  sut.toDoItem = toDoItem

  XCTAssertEqual(sut.locationLabel.text, location)
}
```

Make these tests pass one by one. Make sure that you never have more than one failing test.

The map view should show a map of the location of the to-do item when the to-do item contains a location with a coordinate. Follow these steps to add that feature:

1. Add the following test to `ToDoItemDetailsViewControllerTests`:

    ```
    // ToDoItemDetailsViewControllerTests.swift
    func test_settingToDoItem_shouldUpdateMapView() {
      let latitude = 51.225556
      let longitude = 6.782778
      let toDoItem = ToDoItem(
        title: "dummy title",
        location: Location(
          name: "dummy location",
          coordinate: Coordinate(latitude: latitude,
            longitude: longitude)))

      sut.toDoItem = toDoItem

      let center = sut.mapView.centerCoordinate
      XCTAssertEqual(center.latitude,
        latitude,
        accuracy: 0.000_01)
      XCTAssertEqual(center.longitude,
    ```

```
        longitude,
        accuracy: 0.000_01)
}
```

With this test, we test if the center coordinate of the map view is set to the coordinate of the location of the to-do item.

Run all tests to confirm that this new test fails.

2. To make this test pass, add the following code to the `didSet` handler of the `toDoItem` property in `ToDoItemDetailsViewController`:

```
// ToDoItemDetailsViewController.swift
if let coordinate = toDoItem?.location?.coordinate {
  mapView.setCenter(
    CLLocationCoordinate2D(
      latitude: coordinate.latitude,
      longitude: coordinate.longitude),
    animated: false)
}
```

Run the tests again to confirm that all tests now pass.

When the presented to-do item is already done, the **Done** button should be disabled. Follow these steps to implement this feature:

1. Add the following test to `ToDoItemDetailsViewControllerTests`:

```
// ToDoItemDetailsViewControllerTests.swift
func test_settingToDoItem_shouldUpdateButtonState() {
  var toDoItem = ToDoItem(title: "dummy title")
  toDoItem.done = true

  sut.toDoItem = toDoItem

  XCTAssertFalse(sut.doneButton.isEnabled)
}
```

Run the tests to confirm that this new test fails.

2. To make this new test pass, add the following code to the didSet handler of the toDoItem property:

```
// ToDoItemDetailsViewController.swift
doneButton.isEnabled = false
```

This code makes the test pass. Try it by running all tests. But this line of code is clearly wrong because it disables the **Done** button for all to-do items, even for those that are not done yet. To fix this bug, we need another test.

3. Add the following test to ToDoItemDetailsViewControllerTests:

```
// ToDoItemDetailsViewControllerTests.swift
func test_settingToDoItem_whenItemNotDone_
  shouldUpdateButtonState() {
    let toDoItem = ToDoItem(title: "dummy title")

    sut.toDoItem = toDoItem

    XCTAssertTrue(sut.doneButton.isEnabled)
}
```

Run the tests. This new test fails.

4. To make it pass, replace the doneButton.isEnabled = false line with the following code:

```
// ToDoItemDetailsViewController.swift
doneButton.isEnabled = (toDoItem?.done == false)
```

Run all tests again to confirm that this code fixes the bug.

Great! We are finished with updating the user interface with the information from the to-do item. In the following section, we will implement the functionality of the **Done** button.

Checking the to-do item

When the user of the app taps the **Done** button, our app has to tell the to-do item store to change the item's status to **Done**. Follow these steps to implement that feature:

1. Add the following test method to `ToDoItemDetailsViewControllerTests`:

    ```swift
    // ToDoItemDetailsViewControllerTest.swift
    func test_sendingButtonAction_shouldCheckItem() {
        let toDoItem = ToDoItem(title: "dummy title")
        sut.toDoItem = toDoItem
        let storeMock = ToDoItemStoreProtocolMock()
        sut.toDoItemStore = storeMock
    }
    ```

    `ToDoItemDetailsViewController` doesn't have a property for `toDoItemStore`. This means we have to pause writing this test and add this property first.

2. Go to `ToDoItemDetailsViewController` and add the `toDoItemStore` property:

    ```swift
    // ToDoItemDetailsViewController.swift
    var toDoItemStore: ToDoItemStoreProtocol?
    ```

3. Now we can finish the test:

    ```swift
    // ToDoItemDetailsViewControllerTests.swift
    func test_sendingButtonAction_shouldCheckItem() {
        let toDoItem = ToDoItem(title: "dummy title")
        sut.toDoItem = toDoItem
        let storeMock = ToDoItemStoreProtocolMock()
        sut.toDoItemStore = storeMock

        sut.doneButton.sendActions(for: .touchUpInside)

        XCTAssertEqual(storeMock.checkLastCallArgument,
            toDoItem)
    }
    ```

With the `sut.doneButton.sendActions(for: .touchUpInside)` call, we send the `.touchUpInside` action to the target of the **Done** button. The test assertion checks if the check method of `toDoItemStore` was called with the `toDoItem` variable of the system under test.

4. To add an action to the **Done** button, open the `Main.storyboard` file and the `ToDoItemDetailsViewController.swift` file side by side. Hold down the *Ctrl* key and drag a connection from the **Done** button into the code:

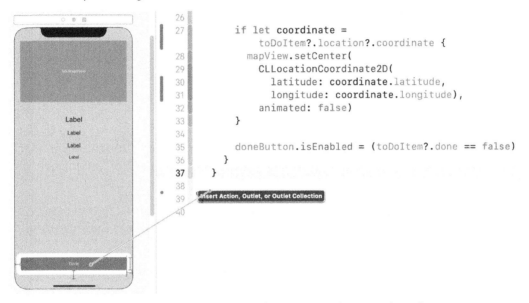

Figure 8.9 – Drag a connection from the Done button to the code

5. Change **Connection** to **Action**, put `checkItem` in the **Name** field, and change **Type** to **UIButton**. Then click **Connect**:

Figure 8.10 – Options for the button action

6. Next, change the action code to the following:

```
// ToDoItemDetailsViewController.swift
@IBAction func checkItem(_ sender: UIButton) {
  if let toDoItem = toDoItem {
    toDoItemStore?.check(toDoItem)
  }
}
```

Run all tests to confirm that this makes all tests pass again.

When the item is checked as **Done**, the **Done** button should be disabled to show the user that this task is finished. You will implement this feature in the exercises for this chapter.

Summary

In this chapter, we built a simple detail view controller following test-driven development. We learned how to test a view controller that is set up using a storyboard. And finally, we figured out what we have to do to test the action of a button.

The skills you gained in this chapter will help you in writing tests for all kinds of user interfaces, even those that are more complicated. You are now able to test the presence and the interaction of user interface elements with the rest of the code.

In the next chapter, we will write tests for a view that is created using SwiftUI. For that task, we will have to add a third-party library from GitHub to our test target.

Exercises

1. When the user selects the **Done** button to show the task as finished, the **Done** button should be disabled to show the user that this action was successful. Implement this feature.

2. Change the code so that the map view is hidden when no coordinate is set in the to-do item.

9
Test-Driven Input View in SwiftUI

In 2019, Apple introduced **SwiftUI** as a new way to build user interfaces for apps on Apple platforms. In contrast to user interfaces built with UIKit, SwiftUI views are a function of some kind of state. As a result, testing such views can be very easy. In a test, we would have to set the state and assert that the expected user interface elements are present.

Unfortunately, the engineers in charge at Apple believe that there is no value in testing user interfaces. They believe that to prove the user interface looks and works as expected, it's enough to run the app and check with your eyes. This might be true for an app as simple as the one we are building in this book. But, if you have a look in the App Store, you will find most of the apps (if not all) are way more complicated. Usually, apps consist of many views and some of them are only visible in some rare cases. Ensuring that those views work for all input values and environment parameters is a lot of work.

Also, think about refactoring. Apps are never finished. We need to change and add features all the time. How do engineers make sure that all previous features still work?

Automatic tests performed by a computer are faster than manual tests by several orders of magnitude. In my opinion, engineers not using automatic tests, even for user interfaces, wastes time and money.

So, what do we do when we want to build a user interface using SwiftUI and still rely on the advantages of test-driven development? Fortunately, there is a third-party library called **ViewInspector** on GitHub that fills this gap. In this chapter, we will add this library to our project and explore how we can write unit tests for SwiftUI code.

This chapter is structured into the following sections:

- Adding the ViewInspector package
- Using ViewInspector to test a simple view
- Testing button actions with ViewInspector

Let's start by adding ViewInspector to our test target.

Technical requirement

The source code for this chapter is available here: `https://github.com/PacktPublishing/Test-Driven-iOS-Development-with-Swift-Fourth-Edition/tree/main/chapter09`.

Adding the ViewInspector package

ViewInspector is an open source library that you can find on GitHub: `https://github.com/nalexn/ViewInspector`. To add it to our project, follow these steps:

1. Select the **File | Add Packages** menu item in Xcode.
2. Type into the search field the URL of the package, `https://github.com/nalexn/ViewInspector`:

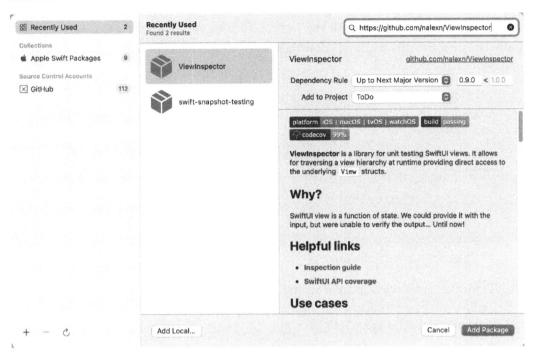

Figure 9.1 – Add the ViewInspector package

Click **Add Package**.

3. Xcode presents a new window in which we can set the target to which the package should be added. Select the **ToDoTests** target. Then click **Add Package** again.

The package is now added to the **ToDoTests** target and we can use it in our unit tests.

Using ViewInspector to test a simple view

The view we are going to build will be used to add new to-do items to the list of items. This means it needs input fields for all information a to-do item can hold. So, let's look into that aspect in the next subsections.

Adding a title text field

As always, we start with the test. Follow these steps to add a text field for the title of a to-do item to the input view:

1. Select the **ToDoTests** group in the project navigator and add a **Unit Test Case Class** with the name `ToDoItemInputViewTests`. Remove the two template test methods.

2. Import the `ViewInspector` library and the main target (`ToDo`) so that it is testable (`@testable`):

```
// ToDoItemInputViewTests.swift
import XCTest
@testable import ToDo
import ViewInspector
```

3. Before we can write tests for a SwiftUI view, we first need to extend it with the `Inspectable` protocol from the `ViewInspector` library. Add the following line right above the test case class:

```
// ToDoItemInputViewTests.swift
extension ToDoItemInputView: Inspectable {}
```

At this point, Xcode complains that it **Cannot find type 'ToDoItemInputView' in scope**. That was expected as we haven't added this type yet.

4. Select the **ToDo** group in the project navigator and add a SwiftUI file:

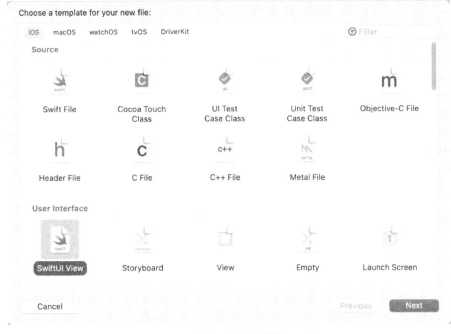

Figure 9.2 – Select the SwiftUI template

5. Put `ToDoItemInputView.swift` in the **Save As** field:

Figure 9.3 – The name of the new file is ToDoItemInputView.swift

Now, the error in the test code is gone and we can continue with the test.

6. Add a property for the system under test and for the data object holding the information for the new to-do item:

```
// ToDoItemInputViewTests.swift
var sut: ToDoItemInputView!
var toDoItemData: ToDoItemData!
```

We will fill `toDoitemData` with the data the user puts into the view, and when they are finished, we will create a `ToDoItem` instance from that data.

Again, Xcode tells us that something is missing.

7. Select the **ToDo** group in the project navigator and add a SwiftUI file with `ToDoItemData` as the name.

8. Replace the contents of this file with the following code:

```
// ToDoItemData.swift
import Foundation


class ToDoItemData: ObservableObject {
}
```

This new type needs to be the `ObservableObject` type because we want to use it as the state of our SwiftUI view.

9. Go back to the `ToDoItemInputViewTests` class and replace `setUpWithError()` and `tearDownWithError()` with the following code:

```
// ToDoItemInputViewTests .swift
override func setUpWithError() throws {
  toDoItemData = ToDoItemData()
  sut = ToDoItemInputView(data: toDoItemData)
}


override func tearDownWithError() throws {
  sut = nil
  toDoItemData = nil
}
```

10. The preceding code does not compile, as the initializer of `ToDoItemInputView` doesn't take any arguments. To fix the compilation error, add the following property to `ToDoItemInputView`:

```
// ToDoItemInputView.swift
@ObservedObject var data: ToDoItemData
```

11. Now, Xcode shows an error in the `ToDoItemInputView_Previews` structure because the new property is missing in the initializer of `ToDoItemInputView`. Replace the contents of the `ToDoItemInputView_Previews` structure with the following code to fix this error:

```
// ToDoItemInputView.swift
static var previews: some View {
    ToDoItemInputView(data: ToDoItemData())
}
```

12. Now, let's get back to the test case class. Add the following fragment of a test method to `ToDoItemInputViewTests`:

```
// ToDoItemInputViewTests.swift
func test_titleInput_shouldSetValueInData() throws {
    let expected = "dummy title"
    try sut
        .inspect()
        .find(ViewType.TextField.self)
        .setInput(expected)

    let input = toDoItemData.title
}
```

The `toDoItemData` type has no `title` property. We will fix this in the next step. But first, let's try to understand what is happening here.

First, we call `inspect()` on the system under test (`sut`). This is possible because we extended the `ToDoItemInputView` call with conformance to the `Inspectable` protocol. On the returned type, we can call the `find` method that returns the first instance of the given type, in this case, the `TextField` type. On the value that is returned from the `find` call, we call `setInput(_:)` to simulate user input to that text field.

13. Add the following `title` property to `ToDoItemData`:

```
// ToDoItemData.swift
@Published var title = ""
```

14. Finish the test with the following `Assert` function call:

```
// ToDoItemInputViewTests.swift
func test_shouldAllowTitleInput() throws {
  let expected = "dummy title"
  try sut
    .inspect()
    .find(ViewType.TextField.self)
    .setInput(expected)

  let input = toDoItemData.title

  XCTAssertEqual(input, expected)
}
```

Run the tests to confirm that this new test fails. The test fails in the line where we try to find the `TextField` element.

15. Replace the content of the `body` property in `ToDoItemInputView` with the following code:

```
// ToDoItemInputView.swift
TextField("Title", text: $data.title)
```

Run the tests again. Now all tests pass but we haven't seen the assertion fail. The test failed previously because it could not find a `TextField` element in the body of the view. Is this a problem? It could be. If we are not careful, we could write an assertion that always passes. So, it is a good idea to change the code in a way that the assertion fails but the rest of the test passes.

16. Replace the `ToDoItemInputView` structure with the following code:

```
// ToDoItemInputView.swift
struct ToDoItemInputView: View {
    @ObservedObject var data: ToDoItemData
    @State var dummy: String = ""

    var body: some View {
        TextField("Title", text: $dummy)
    }
}
```

Here we have added a dummy variable to act as the binding for the text of `TextField`. Run the tests to confirm that the last added test now fails at the assertion. As we have checked that the assertion can fail, we can change the code so that the test passes again.

That was easy. With the help of `ViewInspector`, we were able to write a test for the input text field of the title for the to-do item.

In the next section, we will add a `DatePicker` structure to allow the user to add due dates to to-do items.

Adding a DatePicker

The title is the only required data of a to-do item. The date is optional. In the user interface of the input view, we want to use a `DatePicker` structure for the input of the date value. We will use a toggle to show the `DatePicker` structure when the user wants to add a date for that to-do item.

This means we first need a test that asserts that the view initially doesn't show a date picker. Add the following test method to `ToDoItemInputView`:

```
// ToDoItemInputViewTests.swift
func test_whenWithoutDate_shouldNotShowDateInput() {
    XCTAssertThrowsError(try sut
        .inspect()
        .find(ViewType.DatePicker.self))
}
```

With this code, we assert that the code in the parameter of the
XCTAssertThrowsError function throws an error. This means we test that there is no
DatePicker in the view. The test fails if the find method finds a DatePicker.

We don't have to do anything to make this test pass. It already passes. We could add a
DatePicker to see it failing. Actually, we will do that next.

The toggle element to show and hide the date picker will be bound to a @State property
with the withDate property defined in ToDoItemInputView. As a result, the state of
the toggle element will be reflected in the value of the withDate property. Interacting
with a @State property from a unit test needs some change of the view code. We will
start the implementation of the date input with the following change:

1. Replace the ToDoItemInputView structure with the following code:

```
// ToDoItemInputView.swift
struct ToDoItemInputView: View {
    @ObservedObject var data: ToDoItemData
    var didAppear: ((Self) -> Void)?

    var body: some View {
        VStack {
            TextField("Title", text: $data.title)
        }
        .onAppear { self.didAppear?(self) }
    }
}
```

We added here a closure with a didAppear name that is called in the onAppear
modifier of the VStack structure. We need a VStack structure or something
similar here because, later in these steps, we will add more elements to the body of
the view.

2. With this preparation we can add the first fragment of the test:

```
// ToDoItemInputViewTests.swift
func test_whenWithDate_shouldAllowDateInput() throws {
    let exp = sut.on(\.didAppear) { view in
        try view.find(ViewType.Toggle.self).tap()

        let expected = Date(timeIntervalSinceNow:
```

```
        1_000_000)
      try view
        .find(ViewType.DatePicker.self)
        .select(date: expected)

      let input = self.toDoItemData.date
    }

    ViewHosting.host(view: sut)
    wait(for: [exp], timeout: 0.1)
  }
```

We start the test method with an expectation. It is needed here to make updating the `@State` property accessible in the test. The reason for that lies in the implementation details of view updates in SwiftUI.

All the communication with the system under test has to be put into the closure of the expectation we define using `sut.on(\.didAppear) {}`.

In the closure, we first switch the toggle to make the date picker appear. Next, we search for the `DatePicker` and we try to set its date. Then we access the date of the `toDoItemDate` property. The test is not finished, but we have to pause here because the `Date` property is missing.

Below the closure, we ask the `ViewInspector` library to host the system under test. This triggers the `onAppear` closure and makes working with `@State` properties possible. Finally, we have to wait for the expectation to be fulfilled. We don't have to call `fulfill()` on the expectation ourselves. This is managed by the `ViewInspector` library.

3. Go to `ToDoItemData` and add the `Date` property:

```
// ToDoItemData.swift
@Published var date = Date()
```

4. Now, we can finish the test by adding the `Assert` function call:

```
// ToDoItemInputView.swift
func test_whenWithDate_shouldAllowDateInput() throws {
  let exp = sut.on(\.didAppear) { view in
    try view.find(ViewType.Toggle.self).tap()
```

```
        let expected = Date(timeIntervalSinceNow:
          1_000_000)
        try view
          .find(ViewType.DatePicker.self)
          .select(date: expected)

        let input = self.toDoItemData.date
        XCTAssertEqual(input, expected)
      }

    ViewHosting.host(view: sut)
    wait(for: [exp], timeout: 0.1)
    }
```

Run all tests to confirm that this new test is failing. It fails because it can't find the toggle. Let's add the toggle in the next step.

5. Add the following property for the state of the toggle we are about to add:

```
// ToDoItemInputView.swift
@State var withDate = false
```

6. Next, replace the contents of the computed body property with the following code:

```
// ToDoItemInputView.swift
VStack {
  TextField("Title", text: $data.title)
  Toggle("Add Date", isOn: $withDate)
}
.onAppear { self.didAppear?(self) }
```

Now the test fails because it can't find the date picker.

7. Add the date picker as follows:

```
// ToDoItemInputView.swift
VStack {
  TextField("Title", text: $data.title)
  Toggle("Add Date", isOn: $withDate)
  DatePicker("Date", selection: $data.date)
```

```
    }
    .onAppear { self.didAppear?(self) }
```

Now, test_whenWithDate_shouldAllowDateInput passes but test_
whenWithoutDate_shouldNotShowDateInput fails. This is a good thing
because we haven't seen this test fail until now.

8. To make both tests pass, replace the code of the computed body property with
    the following:

```
// ToDoItemInputView.swift
var body: some View {
  VStack {
    TextField("Title", text: $data.title)
    Toggle("Add Date", isOn: $withDate)
    if withDate {
      DatePicker("Date", selection: $data.date)
    }
  }
  .onAppear { self.didAppear?(self) }
}
```

Run all tests to confirm that all tests pass again.

In making the last test pass, we learned what we have to do to test changes where a
@State property is involved. This was shown here because you need to know this
when you start writing tests for SwiftUI views.

Now that we have seen how to test changes to @State properties, let's refactor the test
code and the implementation to make both easier to understand.

Improving the test code and the implementation

For our app, it would be better if we move the withDate property to ToDoItemData
because we need this information when we try to create the to-do item. Follow these steps
to move that property to ToDoItemData:

1. Go to ToDoItemInputTests and replace test_whenWithDate_
    shouldAllowDateInput() with the following implementation:

```
// ToDoItemInputTests.swift
func test_whenWithDate_shouldAllowDateInput() throws {
  let expected = Date()
```

```
try sut.inspect().find(ViewType.Toggle.self).tap()
try sut
    .inspect()
    .find(ViewType.DatePicker.self)
    .select(date: expected)

let input = toDoItemData.date

XCTAssertEqual(input, expected)
}
```

Run all tests. This test now fails because we can't interact with a `@State` property this way.

2. Delete the `@State var withDate = false` line from `ToDoItemInputView`.

3. Go to `ToDoItemData` and add the following property:

```
// ToDoItemData.swift
@Published var withDate = false
```

4. Now in `ToDoItemInputView`, replace all occurrences of `withDate` with `data.withDate`:

```
// ToDoItemInputView.swift
var body: some View {
  VStack {
    TextField("Title", text: $data.title)
    Toggle("Add Date", isOn: $data.withDate)
    if data.withDate {
      DatePicker("Date", selection: $data.date)
    }
  }
}
```

Note that we have removed the `.onAppear` call below the closing brace of `VStack`. As it is not needed anymore, you can also remove the `didAppear` property from `ToDoItemInputView`.

Run all tests to confirm that all tests now pass again.

We now have an input view for the title and the date of a to-do item. Next, we need a text field for the item description.

Adding another text field

Follow these steps to add another text field to the input view:

1. Go to `ToDoItemInputViewTests` and add the following incomplete test method:

```
// ToDoItemInputViewTests.swift
func test_shouldAllowDescriptionInput() throws {
  let expected = "dummy description"
  try sut
    .inspect()
    .find(ViewType.TextField.self,
      where: { view in
      let label = try view
        .labelView()
        .text()
        .string()
      return label == "Description"
    })
    .setInput(expected)

    let input = toDoItemData.itemDescription
  }
```

This looks similar to the test we wrote for the `title` property, but this time we have to specify which `TextField` we are searching for. We added a `where` closure to find the text field with a `Description` label text. Within the `where` closure, we use the inspection capabilities of `ViewInspector` to find the string of the text of `labelView` of `TextField`.

2. The test does not compile, because the `itemDescription` property is missing in `ToDoItemData`. Add the property as shown in the following code:

```
// ToDoItemData.swift
class ToDoItemData: ObservableObject {
  @Published var title = ""
```

```
@Published var date = Date()
@Published var withDate = false
@Published var itemDescription = ""
}
```

3. Now we can finish the test. Add the following assertion to the test:

```
// ToDoItemInputViewTests.swift
XCTAssertEqual(input, expected)
```

Run the tests to confirm that this new test fails.

4. Go to ToDoItemInputView and change the body property so that it looks as follows:

```
// ToDoItemInputView.swift
var body: some View {
  VStack {
    TextField("Title", text: $data.title)
    Toggle("Add Date", isOn: $data.withDate)
    if data.withDate {
      DatePicker("Date", selection: $data.date)
    }
    TextField("Description",
      text: $data.itemDescription)
  }
}
```

Run the tests to confirm that all tests pass.

Here, we could again change the code to see the assertion of the test fail, as we did for the test of the title property. As the code and the test code look similar, I'm confident in the test without doing that. Think for yourself if you would like to see the assertion fail.

To make the test for the title property more robust against changes in the user interface, add a similar where closure to test_shouldAllowTitleInput.

A to-do item can also have a location associated with it. This means we need another text field for the location name. You have already seen how to add a text field to the input view, so this is left to you as an exercise. Use the locationName property name in ToDoItemData and the "Location name" title for the title of TextField.

Before we move on, let's make the user interface a bit nicer.

Improving the user interface

Right now, the text fields and the date picker are structured using a VStack structure. This is the easiest, but not the prettiest way to do it. The user interface of the input view looks like this at the moment:

Figure 9.4 – The user interface of the input view when using a VStack

We can improve the user interface by using Form and Section structures. Replace the body property code of ToDoItemInput with the following:

```
// ToDoItemInput.swift
var body: some View {
  Form {
    SwiftUI.Section {
      TextField("Title", text: $data.title)
      Toggle("Add Date", isOn: $data.withDate)
      if data.withDate {
        DatePicker("Date", selection: $data.date)
      }
      TextField("Description",
        text: $data.itemDescription)
    }
    SwiftUI.Section {
      TextField("Location name",
        text: $data.locationName)
    }
```

```
    }


 }
```

We have to specify in this code that we want `Section` defined in SwiftUI because we already defined a section type. With this code, the user interface looks as follows:

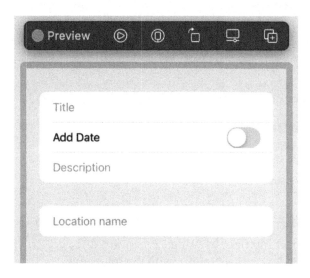

Figure 9.5 – An improved user interface with Form and Section

This looks way better. Run the tests to confirm that we didn't break something.

In the next section, we will add another text field and a button.

Adding an address text field and a button

We need another text field for the address of the to-do item. Use your gained experience to add it yourself to the location section of the input form. To make your code consistent with the code of the book on GitHub, name the property `addressString` in `ToDoItemData` and use the label `Address` in the `TextField` type.

After entering the data for the to-do item, the user can add it to the list. For that task, we need a button in the user interface. Follow these steps to add the button:

1. Add the following test to `ToDoItemInputViewTests`:

```
// ToDoItemInputViewTests.swift
func test_shouldHaveASaveButton() throws {
    XCTAssertNoThrow(try sut
```

```
        .inspect()
        .find(ViewType.Button.self,
          where: { view in
          let label = try view
            .labelView()
            .text()
            .string()
          return label == "Save"
        }))
  }
```

Run the tests to see this new test fail.

2. Add the following code within the Form of the body property of
    ToDoItemInputView:

```
// ToDoItemInputView.swift
SwiftUI.Section {
  Button(action: addToDoItem,
    label: {
    Text("Save")
  })
}
```

3. To make this code compile, we need to add the action. Add the following method to
    ToDoItemInputView below the body property:

```
// ToDoItemInputView.swift
func addToDoItem() {
}
```

Run all tests to confirm that all tests now pass.

Now we have all the user interface elements needed to move on to implementing adding
the to-do item to the list of items in the next section.

Testing button actions with ViewInspector

The user puts in the address for the to-do item. In the details view of an item, the app shows a map of that location. This means we need to convert the address of the item to a coordinate before we can add the item to the list. Apple provides a `GeoCoder` class for that task. We will write tests for fetching an address from a `GeoCoder` class in *Chapter 10, Testing Networking Code*.

In this chapter, we assume that we already have a class called `APIClient` that uses `GeoCoder` (or some similar service) to translate an address into a coordinate. In the test, we are going to use a mock object for that `APIClient` class. Follow these steps to add a protocol for the `APIClient` class and a mock conforming to that protocol:

1. Select the **ToDo** group in the project navigator and add a new Swift file with the name `APIClient.swift`.

2. Add the following protocol definition to that new file:

```
// APIClient.swift
protocol APIClientProtocol {
  func coordinate(
    for: String,
    completion: (Coordinate?) -> Void)
}
```

This protocol defines a function that takes a `String` instance and calls a `completion` handler with a `Coordinate` instance.

3. Select the **ToDoTests** group in the project navigator and add a new Swift file with the name `APIClientMock.swift`.

4. Replace the contents of that file with the following code:

```
// APIClientMock.swift
import Foundation
@testable import ToDo

class APIClientMock: APIClientProtocol {
  var coordinateAddress: String?
  var coordinateReturnValue: Coordinate?

  func coordinate(
    for address: String,
```

```
        completion: (Coordinate?) -> Void) {
            coordinateAddress = address
            completion(coordinateReturnValue)
    }
}
```

With this mock in place, we can write a test that asserts that the `coordinate` instance is fetched when the user taps the **Save** button. Follow these steps to add that test and the implementation that makes the test pass:

1. Add a new property (`apiClientMock`) to the `ToDoItemInputViewTests` class:

    ```
    // ToDoItemInputViewTests.swift
    var apiClientMock: APIClientMock!
    ```

2. In `setUpWithError`, initialize an API client mock and pass it into the initializer of `ToDoItemInputView`:

    ```
    // ToDoItemInputViewTests.swift
    override func setUpWithError() throws {
        toDoItemData = ToDoItemData()
        apiClientMock = APIClientMock()
        sut = ToDoItemInputView(
            data: toDoItemData,
            apiClient: apiClientMock)
    }
    ```

3. Don't forget to set this property to `nil` in `tearDownWithError`:

    ```
    // ToDoItemInputViewTests.swift
    override func tearDownWithError() throws {
        sut = nil
        toDoItemData = nil
        apiClientMock = nil
    }
    ```

`ToDoItemInputView` doesn't have a property for the API client. We need to add it before we can continue with the test.

4. Add the `apiClient` property to `ToDoItemInputView`:

```
// ToDoItemInputView.swift:
let apiClient: APIClientProtocol
```

As `ToDoItemInputView` is a structure, this new property changes
the automatically generated initializer. We use this initializer in
`ToDoItemInputView_Previews` in the same file.

5. Replace the `ToDoItemInputView_Previews` structure with the
following implementation:

```
// ToDoItemInputView.swift
struct ToDoItemInputView_Previews: PreviewProvider {
  static var previews: some View {
    ToDoItemInputView(data: ToDoItemData(),
      apiClient: APIClient())
      .previewLayout(.sizeThatFits)
  }
}
```

With this code, we replaced the error with another. The implementation of
`APIClient` is missing.

6. Add the following minimal implementation to `APIClient.swift`:

```
// APIClient.swift
class APIClient: APIClientProtocol {
  func coordinate(
    for: String,
    completion: (Coordinate?) -> Void) {
  }
}
```

7. Now we can add the test method:

```
// ToDoItemInputViewTests.swift
func test_saveButton_shouldFetchCoordinate() throws {
  toDoItemData.title = "dummy title"
  let expected = "dummy address"
  toDoItemData.addressString = expected
```

```
try sut
  .inspect()
  .find(ViewType.Button.self,
        where: { view in
  let label = try view
    .labelView()
    .text()
    .string()
  return label == "Save"
})
  .tap()


XCTAssertEqual(apiClientMock.coordinateAddress,
  expected)
}
```

In this test, we set up the title and the address of the input data and tap the **Save** button. We expect that this fetches the `coordinate` instances for the address.

Run the tests to confirm that this new test fails.

8. Replace the `addToDoItem()` method in `ToDoItemInputView` with the following implementation:

```
// ToDoItemInputView.swift
func addToDoItem() {
  apiClient.coordinate(
    for: data.addressString,
      completion: { coordinate in
  })
}
```

In this implementation, we call the `coordinate(for:completion:)` method defined in `APIClientProtocol`.

Run the tests to confirm that all tests now pass.

9. But what if the user didn't add an address to the input form? In this case, the
    `coordinate(for:completion:)` method should not be called because there
    is no coordinate to be fetched. We need a test for this case. Add the following test to
    `ToDoInputViewTests.swift`:

```
// ToDoInputViewTests.swift
func test_save_whenAddressEmpty_
   shouldNotFetchCoordinate() throws {
   toDoItemData.title = "dummy title"

   try sut
      .inspect()
      .find(ViewType.Button.self,
         where: { view in
      let label = try view
         .labelView()
         .text()
         .string()
      return label == "Save"
   })
      .tap()

   XCTAssertNil(apiClientMock.coordinateAddress)
}
```

Run all tests to confirm that this new test fails.

10. To make it pass, change the code in `addToDoItem()` so that it looks like this:

```
// ToDoItemInputView.swift
func addToDoItem() {
   if false == data.addressString.isEmpty {
      apiClient.coordinate(
         for: data.addressString,
         completion: { coordinate in
            })
   }
}
```

Run all tests to confirm that all tests pass.

After the `coordinate` has been fetched, the `addToDoItem()` method should call a delegate method to inform it that the input data is complete and the item can be constructed. Again, we will add a `delegate` protocol to define the interface of the `delegate` object. This helps when we create a mock object for the test.

Follow these steps to add the tests and the implementation of calling the `delegate` protocol with the to-do item data:

1. Add the following protocol definition to `ToDoItemInputView.swift` outside of the `ToDoItemInputView` structure:

```
// ToDoItemInputView.swift
protocol ToDoItemInputViewDelegate {
  func addToDoItem(with: ToDoItemData,
    coordinate: Coordinate?)
}
```

2. With this protocol in place, we can add a mock object to the test target. Select the `ToDoTests` group in the project navigator and add a Swift file with the name `ToDoItemInputViewDelegateMock.swift`. Add the following code to this new file:

```
// ToDoItemInputViewDelegateMock.swift
import Foundation
@testable import ToDo

class ToDoItemInputViewDelegateMock:
  ToDoItemInputViewDelegate {

  var lastToDoItemData: ToDoItemData?
  var lastCoordinate: Coordinate?

  func addToDoItem(with data: ToDoItemData,
    coordinate: Coordinate?) {

    lastToDoItemData = data
    lastCoordinate = coordinate
  }
}
```

3. Now we can start with the test. Add the following test fragment to `ToDoItemInputViewTests`:

```
// ToDoItemInputViewTests.swift
func test_save_shouldCallDelegate() throws {
    toDoItemData.title = "dummy title"
    toDoItemData.addressString = "dummy address"
    apiClientMock.coordinateReturnValue =
    Coordinate(latitude: 1, longitude: 2)
    let delegateMock = ToDoItemInputViewDelegateMock()
    sut.delegate = delegateMock
}
```

Here we set up the `apiClientMock` property to return a dummy coordinate when `coordinate(for:completion:)` is called, and we create an instance of `ToDoItemInputViewDelegateMock` and set it to the `delegate` property of the system under test. This property is still missing and therefore, we have to pause writing the test and first add it to `ToDoItemInputView`.

4. Add this `delegate` property to `ToDoItemInputView`:

```
// ToDoItemInputView.swift
var delegate: ToDoItemInputViewDelegate?
```

This change makes the test compile and we can continue writing the test.

5. Complete the test method so that it looks as follows:

```
// ToDoItemInputViewTests.swift
func test_save_shouldCallDelegate() throws {
    toDoItemData.title = "dummy title"
    toDoItemData.addressString = "dummy address"
    apiClientMock.coordinateReturnValue =
    Coordinate(latitude: 1, longitude: 2)
    let delegateMock = ToDoItemInputViewDelegateMock()
    sut.delegate = delegateMock

    try sut
        .inspect()
        .find(ViewType.Button.self,
            where: { view in
```

```
        let label = try view
            .labelView()
            .text()
            .string()
        return label == "Save"
      })
      .tap()

    XCTAssertEqual(delegateMock.lastToDoItemData?.title,
        "dummy title")
    XCTAssertEqual(delegateMock.lastCoordinate?
        .latitude, 1)
    XCTAssertEqual(delegateMock.lastCoordinate?
        .longitude, 2)
}
```

Usually, I try to keep all the relevant code in the test. But in this case, the test method is a bit messy. As an example, let's move the inspector code into a method.

6. Add the following extension in `ToDoItemInputViewTests.swift` below the `ToDoItemInputViewTests` class:

```
// ToDoItemInputViewTests.swift
extension ToDoItemInputView {
  func tapButtonWith(name: String) throws {
    try inspect()
      .find(ViewType.Button.self,
        where: { view in
        let label = try view
            .labelView()
            .text()
            .string()
        return label == name
      })
      .tap()
  }
}
```

7. With this extension we can write the last test as follows:

```
// ToDoItemInputViewTests.swift
func test_save_shouldCallDelegate() throws {
  toDoItemData.title = "dummy title"
  toDoItemData.addressString = "dummy address"
  apiClientMock.coordinateReturnValue =
  Coordinate(latitude: 1, longitude: 2)
  let delegateMock = ToDoItemInputViewDelegateMock()
  sut.delegate = delegateMock

  try sut.tapButtonWith(name: "Save")

  XCTAssertEqual(delegateMock.lastToDoItemData?.title,
    "dummy title")
  XCTAssertEqual(delegateMock.lastCoordinate?
    .latitude, 1)
  XCTAssertEqual(delegateMock.lastCoordinate?
    .longitude, 2)
}
```

In this case, this is a bit better than the original version.

8. To make this test pass, replace the implementation of addToDoItem() with the following code:

```
// ToDoItemInputView.swift
func addToDoItem() {
  if false == data.addressString.isEmpty {
    apiClient.coordinate(
      for: data.addressString,
        completion: { coordinate in
          self.delegate?.addToDoItem(
            with: data,
            coordinate: coordinate)
        })
  }
}
```

In the completion closure, we now call the `addToDoItem(with:coordinate:)` method.

Run the tests to confirm that this change makes all tests pass.

9. But what if the user didn't add an address for the to-do item? Add the following test to make sure that, in this case, the `delegate` method also gets called:

```
// ToDoItemInputViewTests.swift
func test_save_whenAddressEmpty_
    shouldCallDelegate() throws {
    toDoItemData.title = "dummy title"
    apiClientMock.coordinateReturnValue =
    Coordinate(latitude: 1, longitude: 2)
    let delegateMock = ToDoItemInputViewDelegateMock()
    sut.delegate = delegateMock

    try sut.tapButtonWith(name: "Save")

    XCTAssertEqual(delegateMock.lastToDoItemData?.title,
        "dummy title")
}
```

Run all tests to confirm that this new test fails.

10. To make this test pass, replace `addToDoItem()` in `ToDoItemInputView` with the following code:

```
// ToDoItemInputView.swift
func addToDoItem() {
    if false == data.addressString.isEmpty {
    apiClient.coordinate(
        for: data.addressString,
            completion: { coordinate in
                self.delegate?.addToDoItem(
                    with: data,
                    coordinate: coordinate)
            })
    } else {
        delegate?.addToDoItem(with: data,
            coordinate: nil)
```

```
        }
    }
```

If the `address` string is empty, we call the `delegate` method without a `coordinate` instance.

Run all tests. All tests pass again.

The input view is now complete and we can move on to implementing some networking code.

Summary

Testing SwiftUI code works a bit differently from testing UIKit code. One reason for this is that SwiftUI itself works completely differently. In addition, Apple doesn't provide a testing framework for SwiftUI code because they believe that user interface code should be tested with UITest.

I don't think that's true. UITest solve a different problem. I believe you should have access to both kinds of tests, and you should choose the right tool for the problem at hand.

Fortunately, with ViewInspector we have a powerful third-party solution that fills this gap. In this chapter, we added it as a SwiftUI package to the unit test target. We used the package to write unit tests for SwiftUI code and build an input view for to-do items following test-driven development.

This way, we learned how to add SwiftUI packages to test targets and how to use this specific SwiftUI package to write tests for things that aren't easily testable without it.

In the next chapter, we will learn how to write unit tests for networking code.

Exercises

1. Add more convenient methods in the extension of `ToDoItemInputView` in `ToDoItemInputViewTests.swift` to make the tests easier to read as we did for `test_save_shouldCallDelegate()`. What are the advantages of these helper methods? What are the disadvantages?

2. When the user provides an address, but `GeoCoder` cannot find the coordinate to that address, the app should show an alert and ask the user if they still want to save the item. Go to the GitHub repository of `ViewInspector` (`https://github.com/nalexn/ViewInspector`) and find out how you can test the presentation of an alert. Then write the test that asserts that the alert is presented and implement that feature.

Section 4 – Networking and Navigation

With the preparation and practice we gained in the first three parts of the book, we can now tackle the unit tests for the network and navigation parts of our app. In addition, we will look into how to make the app finally run and work on an iOS simulator.

In this section, we will cover the following chapters:

10

Testing Networking Code

Almost all iOS apps communicate with some kind of server to synchronize data to other devices or to provide additional features that are not possible on the iOS device alone. As the code of the server application is separate from the code of the iOS application, the unit tests for the iOS app should not test features implemented in the server application. The unit tests for the iOS app should only fail if the code of the iOS app has bugs.

To achieve that, the unit tests need to be independent of the server application. This separation has several advantages. The main ones are as follows:

- The unit tests are faster when they don't need to wait for the responses of the server.

- The unit tests do not fail because the server is not available.

- The networking code can be developed using test-driven development, even before the server application is available.

In this chapter, we will implement two different kinds of networking code using test-driven development and mock objects. After you have worked through this chapter, you will be able to write tests for code that communicates with `CLGeoCoder`. You will also learn how to write tests for networking code using the new async/await API of `URLSession`.

This chapter is structured as follows:

- Mocking `CLGeoCoder`
- Testing async/await code that communicates with a `URLSession` instance
- Handling errors

Writing tests for networking code is exciting, so let's get started.

Mocking CLGeoCoder

`CLGeoCoder` is a class provided by Apple that helps you to get coordinates from an address string and vice versa. The methods in `CLGeoCoder` are based on completion closures. In this chapter, we will explore how to mock and test such methods.

Cleaning your project

Before we write the first test for this chapter, let's clean up the project a bit. Add sections in the project navigator and move the files to those sections according to your structure scheme. For inspiration, here is the structure I use for the main target:

Figure 10.1 – Adding structure in the project navigator

Your structure can be completely different. Use the structure you usually use in iOS projects. Also, add a similar structure to the files in the test target.

When you add new files to the project, you have to choose the correct folder depending on the structure you applied.

Preparations for the tests

Before we can write tests for the `APIClient` class we added in *Chapter 9, Test-Driven Input View in SwiftUI*, we need a new test case class. Follow these steps to add it:

1. Add a new **Unit Test Case Class** file with the **Class** name `APIClientTests` to the test target. Remove the two test template methods.

2. Import the `ToDo` module using the `@testable` keyword and add setup and teardown code to the `TestCase` class:

```swift
// APIClientTests.swift
import XCTest
@testable import ToDo

class APIClientTests: XCTestCase {

  var sut: APIClient!

  override func setUpWithError() throws {
    sut = APIClient()
  }

  override func tearDownWithError() throws {
    sut = nil
  }
}
```

Creating the first test

With this preparation, we are ready to write the first test for the `APIClient` class. Follow these steps to add a test for fetching the coordinate of an address using a `CLGeoCoder` instance and make it pass:

1. To be able to replace `CLGeoCoder` in the `APIClient` class with a mock object, we need to define the interface we expect in a protocol. Import the `CoreLocation` framework to `APIClient.swift` and add the following protocol definition to `APIClient.swift` outside of the `APIClient` class implementation:

```
// APIClient.swift
protocol GeoCoderProtocol {
  func geocodeAddressString(
    _ addressString: String,
    completionHandler:
    @escaping CLGeocodeCompletionHandler)
}
```

2. Next, we need to tell the compiler that `CLGeoCoder` already conforms to that protocol. It does so because it already implements a method with this exact signature. Add this line below the `GeoCoderProtocol` implementation:

```
// APIClient.swift
extension CLGeocoder: GeoCoderProtocol {}
```

3. Now, we can define a mock object we will use in the test. Add a new Swift file to the test target and call it `GeoCoderProtocolMock.swift`. Replace its content with the following:

```
// GeoCoderProtocolMock.swift
import Foundation
@testable import ToDo
import CoreLocation

class GeoCoderProtocolMock: GeoCoderProtocol {
  var geocodeAddressString: String?
  var completionHandler: CLGeocodeCompletionHandler?

  func geocodeAddressString(
    _ addressString: String,
```

```
        completionHandler:
        @escaping CLGeocodeCompletionHandler) {
            geocodeAddressString = addressString
            self.completionHandler = completionHandler
    }
}
```

4. In the test, we want to call the
    geocodeAddressString(_:completionHandler:) method and pass a
    CLPlacemark instance into the completion handler. To create a CLPlacemark
    instance in a test, we need to import the Intents and Contacts frameworks,
    because the initializer we need is defined in the Intents framework and uses
    classes from the Contacts framework (I got this tip from the *StackOverflow*
    answer found at https://stackoverflow.com/a/52932708/498796):

```
// APIClientTests.swift
import Intents
import Contacts
```

5. Now, we can start with writing the tests. Add the following fragment of a test to
    APIClientTests:

```
// APIClientTests.swift
func test_coordinate_fetchesCoordinate() {
    let geoCoderMock = GeoCoderProtocolMock()
    sut.geoCoder = geoCoderMock
}
```

Xcode tells us that we need to add a property for the geoCoder property
to APIClient.

6. Go to the APIClient class and add the following property:

```
// APIClient.swift
lazy var geoCoder: GeoCoderProtocol
    = CLGeocoder()
```

The lazy keyword means that the initializer is called the first time the property
is accessed.

7. Go back to the test and make it look like this:

```
// APIClientTests.swift
func test_coordinate_fetchesCoordinate() {
    let geoCoderMock = GeoCoderProtocolMock()
    sut.geoCoder = geoCoderMock
    let location = CLLocation(latitude: 1,
        longitude: 2)
    let placemark = CLPlacemark(location: location,
        name: nil,
        postalAddress: nil)
    let expectedAddress = "dummy address"

    var result: Coordinate?
    sut.coordinate(for: expectedAddress) { coordinate in
        result = coordinate
    }
    geoCoderMock.completionHandler?([placemark], nil)

    XCTAssertEqual(geoCoderMock.geocodeAddressString,
        expectedAddress)
    XCTAssertEqual(result?.latitude,
        location.coordinate.latitude)
    XCTAssertEqual(result?.longitude,
        location.coordinate.longitude)
}
```

After we have set up the `geoCoderMock` instance, we create
dummy variables and call the method we want to test. The
`GeoCoderProtocolMock` class captures the completion handler of the
`geocodeAddressString(_:complectionHandler:)` call. This allows us
to call this completion handler with a placemark we created. In the test assertions,
we check whether the method was called with the address string we provided
and whether the coordinate was passed into the `completion` closure of the
`coordinate(for:completion:)` method.

8. Replace the implementation of coordinate(for:completion:) in APIClient with the following implementation:

```
// APIClient.swift
func coordinate(
  for address: String,
  completion: (Coordinate?) -> Void) {
    geoCoder.geocodeAddressString(
      address) { placemarks, error in
      }
}
```

Note that we added an internal name for the address string parameter.

Run the tests. The new test still fails, but the first assertion doesn't fail anymore. This tells us that our test does too much. We should split this test into two tests: one that checks whether the method is called with the address string we provide, and another one that checks that the coordinate is passed into the completion closure.

9. We should always only have one failing test, so add x_ in front of the method name of test_coordinate_fetchesCoordinate:

```
// APIClientTests.swift
func x_test_coordinate_fetchesCoordinate() {
  // …
```

As the test runner searches for methods beginning with the word test, adding x_ hides the method from the test runner. To confirm that this is true, run all tests again.

10. Now, add the following test method to APIClientTests:

```
// APIClientTests.swift
func test_coordinate_shouldCallGeoCoderWithAddress() {
  let geoCoderMock = GeoCoderProtocolMock()
  sut.geoCoder = geoCoderMock
  let expectedAddress = "dummy address"

  sut.coordinate(for: expectedAddress) { _ in
  }
```

```
XCTAssertEqual(geoCoderMock.geocodeAddressString,
   expectedAddress)
}
```

11. Remove the code we added to `coordinate(for:completion:)` in `APIClient` and run the tests to see this new test fail.

12. Add the code again and run the tests. All tests should pass now.

13. Now, we can remove the check for the address string from `test_coordinate_fetchesCoordinate()` because it is now asserted in `test_coordinate_shouldCallGeoCoderWithAddress()`:

```swift
// APIClientTests.swift
func test_coordinate_fetchesCoordinate() {
   let geoCoderMock = GeoCoderProtocolMock()
   sut.geoCoder = geoCoderMock
   let location = CLLocation(latitude: 1,
      longitude: 2)
   let placemark = CLPlacemark(location: location,
      name: nil,
      postalAddress: nil)

   var result: Coordinate?
   sut.coordinate(for: "") { coordinate in
      result = coordinate
   }
   geoCoderMock.completionHandler?([placemark], nil)

   XCTAssertEqual(result?.latitude,
      location.coordinate.latitude)
   XCTAssertEqual(result?.longitude,
      location.coordinate.longitude)
}
```

Run all tests to see this test fail.

14. To make this test pass, we need to get the coordinate from the CLGeoCoder instance and pass it into the completion handler. Replace the coordinate(for:completion:) method with the following implementation:

```
// APIClient.swift
func coordinate(
  for address: String,
  completion: @escaping (Coordinate?) -> Void) {
    geoCoder.geocodeAddressString(address) {
      placemarks, error in
      guard let clCoordinate =
        placemarks?.first?.location?.coordinate
      else {
        completion(nil)
        return
      }

      let coordinate = Coordinate(
        latitude: clCoordinate.latitude,
        longitude: clCoordinate.longitude)
      completion(coordinate)
    }
  }
```

Now, Xcode complains that **Type 'APIClient' does not conform to protocol 'APIClientProtocol'**. To fix this error, we need to add the @escaping keyword to the completion parameter in the APIClientProtocol protocol.

15. Replace the APIClientProtocol definition with the following:

```
// APIClient.swift
protocol APIClientProtocol {
  func coordinate(
    for: String,
    completion: @escaping (Coordinate?) -> Void)
}
```

16. Run all tests to confirm that now all tests pass.

With this implementation, our app can now fetch the coordinate of an address string. This feature enables our users to add a location to a to-do item.

In the next section, we will implement fetching to-do items from a server. We don't need an actual server to write the tests and the implementation for this feature. This is one of the many advantages of test-driven development.

Testing async/await code that communicates with URLSession

In 2021, Apple introduced async/await in Swift. With async/await, asynchronous code (for example, fetching information from a server) is easier to write and easier to understand. In this section, we will learn how to implement fetching data from a web server using the async/await APIs of the URLSession class; and we will do this, of course, using test-driven development.

Unit tests need to be fast and repeatable. This means we don't want to rely on a connection to a real server in our unit tests. Instead, we will replace the communication with the server with a mock object.

Follow these steps to implement fetching to-do items from a server:

1. In the test, we will use a mock object of a URLSession class instead of the real URLSession instance. To be able to replace the real URLSession instance with the mock, we need a protocol that defines the interface we want to replace.

2. Add the following protocol definition to APIClient.swift:

```
// APIClient.swift
protocol URLSessionProtocol {
  func data(for request: URLRequest,
    delegate: URLSessionTaskDelegate?)
  async throws -> (Data, URLResponse)
}
```

3. Next, we need to tell the compiler that the URLSession class already conforms to this protocol. Add the following code to APIClient.swift:

```
// APIClient.swift
extension URLSession: URLSessionProtocol {}
```

4. Select the **ToDoTests** group in the project navigator and add a new Swift file and call it `URLSessionProtocolMock`. Replace its contents with the following:

```swift
// URLSessionProtoclMock.swift
import Foundation
@testable import ToDo

class URLSessionProtocolMock: URLSessionProtocol {
  var dataForDelegateReturnValue: (Data, URLResponse)?
  var dataForDelegateRequest: URLRequest?

  func data(for request: URLRequest,
    delegate: URLSessionTaskDelegate?)
  async throws -> (Data, URLResponse) {

    dataForDelegateRequest = request

    guard let dataForDelegateReturnValue =
      dataForDelegateReturnValue else {
        fatalError()
        }
    return dataForDelegateReturnValue
  }
}
```

This mock object allows us to define the return value of `data(for:delegate:)` in the test we are going to write.

5. With this preparation, we can start writing the test. Add the following fragment of the test method to `APIClientTests`:

```swift
// APIClientTests.swift
func test_toDoItems_shouldFetcheItems() async throws {
  let url = try XCTUnwrap
    (URL(string: "http://toodoo.app/items"))
  let urlSessionMock = URLSessionProtocolMock()
  let expected = [ToDoItem(title: "dummy title")]
  urlSessionMock.dataForDelegateReturnValue = (
    try JSONEncoder().encode(expected),
```

```
    HTTPURLResponse(url: url,
      statusCode: 200,
      httpVersion: "HTTP/1.1",
      headerFields: nil)!
  )
  sut.session = urlSessionMock
}
```

In this code, we define the URL and the data to be used in the mock response. The urlSessionMock class returns a JSON object with one ToDoItem object and an HTTPURLResponse instance with the expected URL and the status code 200.

We have to pause writing the test because the system under test (the APIClient class) doesn't have a session property yet.

6. Go to APIClient and add the property like this:

```
// APIClient.swift
lazy var session: URLSessionProtocol
= URLSession.shared
```

7. Switch back to the test class and add the call to fetch the to-do items:

```
// APIClientTests.swift
func test_toDoItems_shouldFetcheItems() async throws {
  let url = try XCTUnwrap
    (URL(string: "http://toodoo.app/items"))
  let urlSessionMock = URLSessionProtocolMock()
  let expected = [ToDoItem(title: "dummy title")]
  urlSessionMock.dataForDelegateReturnValue = (
    try JSONEncoder().encode(expected),
    HTTPURLResponse(url: url,
      statusCode: 200,
      httpVersion: "HTTP/1.1",
      headerFields: nil)!
  )
  sut.session = urlSessionMock

  let items = try await sut.toDoItems()
}
```

Again, we have to pause because this method is not defined yet.

8. Go to `APIClient` and add the minimal implementation to make the test compile:

```
// APIClient.swift
func toDoItems() async throws -> [ToDoItem] {
  return []
}
```

9. Finally, we can finish the test. Add the assertion call as shown in this code snippet:

```
// APIClientTests.swift
func test_toDoItems_shouldFetcheItems() async throws {
  let url = try XCTUnwrap
    (URL(string: "http://toodoo.app/items"))
  let urlSessionMock = URLSessionProtocolMock()
  let expected = [ToDoItem(title: "dummy title")]
  urlSessionMock.dataForDelegateReturnValue = (
    try JSONEncoder().encode(expected),
    HTTPURLResponse(url: url,
      statusCode: 200,
      httpVersion: "HTTP/1.1",
      headerFields: nil)!
  )
  sut.session = urlSessionMock

  let items = try await sut.toDoItems()

  XCTAssertEqual(items, expected)
}
```

Run the tests to confirm that this new test fails.

10. To make the test pass, replace the `toDoItems` method in the `APIClient` class with the following code:

```
// APIClient.swift
func toDoItems() async throws -> [ToDoItem] {
  guard let url =
    URL(string: "dummy")
  else {
```

```
    return []
}
let request = URLRequest(url: url)
let (data, _) = try await session.data(
  for: request,
    delegate: nil)
let items = try JSONDecoder()
  .decode([ToDoItem].self, from: data)
return items
}
```

In this code, we define the URL, create a request, call data(for:delegate:) on the session property, and try to decode the result into an array of ToDoItems.

Run the tests to confirm that this code makes the tests pass.

But, there is something strange with this code. The URL is wrong. We need to expand the test to also check for the used URL.

11. Add the following assert function call to the end of test_doToItems_shouldFetchesItems:

```
// APIClientTests.swift
XCTAssertEqual(urlSessionMock.dataForDelegateRequest,
  URLRequest(url: url))
```

Run the tests to confirm that the test now fails because we used the wrong URL in the implementation.

12. To make the test pass, replace the URL initialization in the toDoItems method with this implementation:

```
// APIClient.swift
guard let url =
  URL(string: "http://toodoo.app/items")
else {
  return []
}
```

Run the tests to confirm that now all tests pass.

Of course, this implementation is just an example to get you started testing network calls. In a real app, you would add authorization to the network calls to ensure that users can only access their to-do items and not the ones of other users.

Fetching data from a web service can go wrong. In the following section, we will test whether the error from the URLSession instance is passed down to the caller of toDoItems.

Handling errors

To test the handling of errors in the URLSession call to the web service, we first need to enhance URLSessionProtocolMock. Follow these steps to test that an error in fetching data is passed down to the caller of the APIClient instance:

1. Add the following property to URLSessionProtocolMock:

   ```
   // URLSessionProtocolMock.swift
   var dataForDelegateError: Error?
   ```

2. Next, add the following handling of the error to the start of data(for:delegate:):

   ```
   // URLSessionProtocolMock.swift
   if let error = dataForDelegateError {
     throw error
   }
   ```

   If there is an error set to the dataForDelegateError property, we throw it before we do anything else in this method.

3. Now, we are ready to add the test method to APIClientTests:

   ```
   // APIClientTests.swift
   func test_toDoItems_whenError_shouldPassError() async
     throws {
     let urlSessionMock = URLSessionProtocolMock()
     let expected = NSError(domain: "", code: 1234)
     urlSessionMock.dataForDelegateError = expected
     sut.session = urlSessionMock

     do {
       _ = try await sut.toDoItems()
       XCTFail()
     } catch {
       let nsError = try XCTUnwrap(error as NSError)
   ```

```
        XCTAssertEqual(nsError, expected)
    }
}
```

In this code, we create an error and assign it to the `dataForDelegateError` property of `urlSessionMock`. Then, we call `sut.toDoItems()` within a `do-catch` block to catch the error we expect from the call. If no error is thrown from `toDoItems()` the test fails with `XCTFail`. Otherwise, we compare the error with the expected value.

Run the tests. All tests pass already. This is bad. As you already learned, in test-driven development we need to see a test fail before we make it green. Otherwise, we can't be sure that the tests can fail. It's easy to write tests that always pass. So, let's make the test fail.

4.   Change the implementation of `data(for:delegate:)` in `URLSessionProtocolMock` so that it looks like this:

```swift
// URLSessionProtocolMock.swift
func data(for request: URLRequest,
  delegate: URLSessionTaskDelegate?)
async throws -> (Data, URLResponse) {

  throw NSError(domain: "dummy", code: 0)

  if let error = dataForDelegateError {
    throw error
  }

  dataForDelegateRequest = request
  guard let dataForDelegateReturnValue =
          dataForDelegateReturnValue else {
            fatalError()
          }
  return dataForDelegateReturnValue
}
```

Run the tests again to confirm that with this change, the new test fails.

5.   Remove the `throw NSError(domain: "dummy", code: 0)` line again and run the tests to see all tests pass again.

With this test, we have confirmed that an error in fetching the data from the web service is passed down to the caller of `toDoItems()`.

But what happens when the data from the web service is not in the format we expect? What should happen in this case? Follow these steps to add a test for this case:

1. Add the following test method to `APIClientTests`:

```
// APIClientTests.swift
func
  test_toDoItems_whenJSONIsWrong_shouldFetcheItems()
  async throws {
    let url = try XCTUnwrap(URL(string: "foo"))
    let urlSessionMock = URLSessionProtocolMock()
    urlSessionMock.dataForDelegateReturnValue = (
      try JSONEncoder().encode("dummy"),
      HTTPURLResponse(url: url,
        statusCode: 200,
        httpVersion: "HTTP/1.1",
        headerFields: nil)!
    )
    sut.session = urlSessionMock

    do {
      _ = try await sut.toDoItems()
      XCTFail()
    } catch {
      XCTAssertTrue(error is Swift.DecodingError)
    }
}
```

The data we return here when `toDoItems` of `urlSessionMock` is called is a JSON object of the `dummy` string. Trying to decode this into an array of `ToDoItem` objects should result in an error of the `Swift.DecodingError` type. This is what the last assertion in the test asserts.

2. Run the tests. Again, all tests pass. And again, we need to change something to see this test fail.

3. Go to `APIClient` and replace `toDoItems()` with the following implementation:

```swift
// APIClient.swift
func toDoItems() async throws -> [ToDoItem] {
  guard let url =
    URL(string: "http://toodoo.app/items")
  else {
    return []
  }
  let request = URLRequest(url: url)
  let (data, _) = try await session.data(
    for: request,
      delegate: nil)
  let items = try? JSONDecoder()
    .decode([ToDoItem].self, from: data)
  return items ?? []
}
```

In this code, we have changed the last three lines of that method. Instead of `try`, we use `try?` when we try to decode the data from the web service. When the data cannot be decoded into an array of `ToDoItem`s, the result is optional and no error is thrown. As a result, we also need to change the `return` value. When the value of the `items` property is `nil`, we return an `empty` array.

Run the tests. The test we added last now fails and we have confirmed that it actually can fail.

4. Change the implementation of `toDoItems()` to what it was before:

```swift
// APIClient.swift
func toDoItems() async throws -> [ToDoItem] {
  guard let url =
    URL(string: "http://toodoo.app/items")
  else {
    return []
  }
  let request = URLRequest(url: url)
  let (data, _) = try await session.data(
    for: request,
      delegate: nil)
  let items = try JSONDecoder()
```

```
        .decode([ToDoItem].self, from: data)
    return items
}
```

Run the tests again to see all tests pass again.

There are many more tests to write for the implementation of this web service call. For example, you should also write tests for cases when the web service answers with an HTTP status code other than 200. These tests are left as an exercise for you. Add tests for this API call until you are confident that this feature does not break unnoticed in the future.

Summary

In this chapter, we have learned how to write tests for calls to CLGeoCoder and how to test the async/await REST API calls of URLSession. We have seen what we need to do in the test method to test whether an error is thrown in an async/await call. In addition, we have learned how to make our network code tests independent from the implementation of server infrastructure. This way we made our tests fast and robust.

You can use the skills gained in this chapter to write tests for the complete network layer of your apps. But you don't have to stop there. The strategies we've covered in this chapter also help to write tests for all kinds of async/await APIs.

In the next chapter, we will put all the code that we wrote up to now together, and finally see the app running on the simulator.

Exercises

1. We have deactivated a test method using the x_ prefix to hide it from the test runner. There are other ways to deactivate a single test. Do some research on the internet to figure these out.

2. In this chapter, we wrote tests for the async/await API of URLSession. But, URLSession also provides an API that uses the delegate pattern and one that uses Combine. Do some research on the internet to find out how to write unit tests for these APIs. Make sure that these tests also run when there is no connection to the server.

11
Easy Navigation with Coordinators

An iOS app is usually a collection of single screens somehow connected to each other. Inexperienced developers often present a view controller from another view controller, because this is easy to implement and it is often shown that way in tutorials and demo code. But, for apps that need to be maintained over a long period of time, we need a pattern that is easier to understand and easier to change.

The **coordinator pattern** is very easy to implement and still manages to decouple the navigation between views of the app from the presentation of the information. In the coordinator pattern, a structure called a coordinator is responsible for navigating between views. View controllers tell the coordinator that the user interacted with the app and the coordinator decides which view controller should become responsible for the screen next.

As a bonus, the coordinator pattern makes testing navigation code simpler and more robust, and as a result, this pattern is a good fit for **test-driven development** (TDD).

The app we are building in this book is a small app with only three screens. The navigation between those three screens can be bundled into one coordinator. In more complicated apps, you would usually use more than one coordinator. To learn more about the coordinator pattern, there are plenty of blog posts on the internet about that topic. You don't need to know anything about that pattern to follow the code in this chapter.

In this chapter, you will learn how to test and implement the navigation between the different views of an app using the coordinator pattern.

The chapter is structured as follows:

- Testing the app's setup
- Navigating to the details
- Navigating to a modal view
- Adding missing parts

Let's start by refactoring the app's setup with the coordinator pattern.

Technical requirement

The source code for this chapter can be found here: `https://github.com/PacktPublishing/Test-Driven-iOS-Development-with-Swift-Fourth-Edition/tree/main/chapter11`.

Testing the app's setup

When our app starts, a coordinator should be instantiated and started. This should result in the presentation of the initial view of our app. Follow these steps to refactor the setup from using a storyboard to using a coordinator:

1. Before we can refactor the setup of the app, we need a test that tells us when we break something. Select the **ToDoTests** group in the project navigator and add a new **Unit Test Case Class** instance with the name `AppSetupTests`.

2. Replace the content of the new class with the following:

```swift
// AppSetupTests.swift
import XCTest
@testable import ToDo

class AppSetupTests: XCTestCase {
    func test_application_shouldSetupRoot() {
        let application = UIApplication.shared
        let scene = application.connectedScenes.first
        as? UIWindowScene
        let root =
```

```
    scene?.windows.first?.rootViewController

    XCTAssert(root is ToDoItemsListViewController)
    }
}
```

In this test, we get the `rootViewController` property of the first window of our app and we check whether it is of the `ToDoItemsListViewController` type.

3. Run the tests to confirm that all tests pass right now. This test passes because the storyboard is set up in a way that the app starts with an instance of the `ToDoItemsListViewController` class.

4. Go to `Main.storyboard` and uncheck the checkbox for **Is Initial View Controller** for the `ToDoItemsListViewController` scene in the attribute inspector.

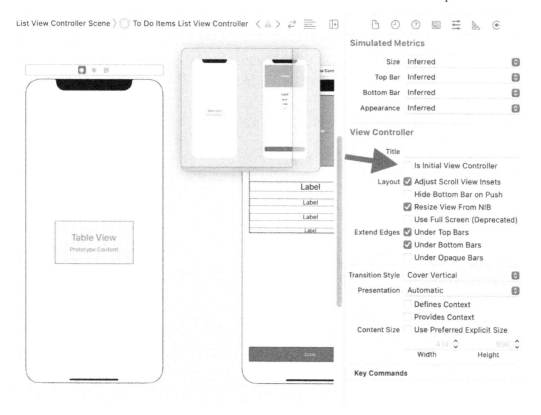

Figure 11.1 – Removing the initial view controller setting from the storyboard

5. Switch to the **Identity** inspector and set **Storyboard ID** to
   `ToDoItemsListViewController`. With this change, we can instantiate this
   view controller in the code using this ID.

6. Run the tests to confirm that now the last test we added fails. Oh, there is another
   test that fails. In `ToDoItemsListViewControllerTests`, all tests fail, because
   the setup in `setUpWithError` throws an error. Let's fix this error before we move
   on with the setup of our app. `ToDoItemsListViewController` isn't the initial
   view controller of the storyboard anymore. This means we need to load it using its
   ID. Replace `setUpWithError()` with the following implementation:

```
// ToDoItemsListViewControllerTests.swift
override func setUpWithError() throws {
  let storyboard = UIStoryboard(name: "Main", bundle:
    nil)
  sut = try XCTUnwrap(
    storyboard.instantiateViewController(
      withIdentifier: "ToDoItemsListViewController")
    as? ToDoItemsListViewController
  )
  toDoItemStoreMock = ToDoItemStoreProtocolMock()
  sut.toDoItemStore = toDoItemStoreMock
  sut.loadViewIfNeeded()
}
```

7. Run all tests again. Now, only our app setup test fails. Good. Let's move on to
   the implementation.

8. Select the **ToDo** group in the project navigator and add a new Swift file with the
   name `AppCoordinator.swift`. Replace the content of the new file with the
   following code:

```
// AppCoordinator.swift
import UIKit


protocol Coordinator {
  func start()
}
```

This code defines the `Coordinator` protocol. This is how I implement the coordinator pattern. In blogs and books of other developers, you might find other implementations. Don't worry, they only differ in their details. When you have worked a bit with the coordinator pattern, you might develop your own implementation.

This implementation of the protocol tells us that a coordinator has a `start` method.

9. Add the following implementation of our `AppCoordinator` in the same file:

```swift
// AppCoordinator.swift
class AppCoordinator: Coordinator {
  private let window: UIWindow?
  private let viewController: UIViewController

  init(window: UIWindow?) {
    self.window = window

    let storyboard = UIStoryboard(name: "Main",
      bundle: nil)
    viewController =
      storyboard.instantiateViewController(
      withIdentifier: "ToDoItemsListViewController")
  }

  func start() {
    window?.rootViewController = viewController
  }
}
```

In the initializer of `AppCoordinator`, we store the window that was passed in as a parameter, and we set up the view of the initial view controller. In the `start` method, we set the `rootViewController` property of the window.

10. Go to `SceneDelegate` and add the following property:

```swift
// SceneDelegate.swift
var appCoordinator: AppCoordinator?
```

11. Next, replace the scene(_:willConnectTo:options:) method with this code:

```
// SceneDelegate.swift
func scene(_ scene: UIScene,
  willConnectTo session: UISceneSession,
  options connectionOptions:
  UIScene.ConnectionOptions) {

  guard let scene = (scene as? UIWindowScene) else {
    return
  }

  window = UIWindow(windowScene: scene)

  let coordinator = AppCoordinator(
    window: window)
  coordinator.start()
  appCoordinator = coordinator

  window?.makeKeyAndVisible()
}
```

In this code, we first set up an instance of the UIWindow class. Next, we instantiate the AppCoordinator instance and call its start method. Finally, we call makeKeyAndVisible on the window to tell UIKit that this window should be presented on the screen.

12. Run all tests to confirm that our refactoring was successful.

Now, the app works as it did before. When the app starts, an instance of ToDoItemsListViewController is created and shown. But, this is not as it should work in the final app. The list of to-do items needs to be presented on a UINavigationController instance to be able to navigate to the details of a to-do item later.

Follow these steps to make this change:

1. Replace the `test_application_shouldSetupRoot()` test method with the following implementation:

```swift
// AppSetupTests.swift
func test_application_shouldSetupRoot() throws {
  let application = UIApplication.shared
  let scene = application.connectedScenes.first
    as? UIWindowScene
  let root = scene?.windows.first?.rootViewController

  let nav = try XCTUnwrap(root as?
    UINavigationController)
  XCTAssert(nav.topViewController
    is ToDoItemsListViewController)
}
```

2. Run the tests to see this test now failing in the line before the `XCTAssert` call.

3. To make this test pass again, we first need a property for the navigation controller in the `AppCoordinator` class:

```swift
// AppCoordinator.swift
private let navigationController:
  UINavigationController
```

4. Next, we set up the navigation controller in the `init` method:

```swift
// AppCoordinator.swift
init(window: UIWindow?,
  navigationController: UINavigationController =
  UINavigationController()) {

  self.window = window
  self.navigationController = navigationController

  let storyboard = UIStoryboard(name: "Main", bundle:
    nil)
```

```
    viewController =
      storyboard.instantiateViewController(
      withIdentifier: "ToDoItemsListViewController")
}
```

We have added the navigation controller as a parameter with a default value to the init call. This will come in handy later when we add tests for the navigation to the details of a to-do item.

5. Now, we can change the start method to add the instance of ToDoItemsListViewController to the navigation stack of the navigation controller:

```
// AppCoordinator.swift
func start() {
  navigationController.pushViewController
    (viewController,
    animated: false)
  window?.rootViewController = navigationController
}
```

Run the tests to confirm that all tests are now passing again.

We are not done yet with setting up the list view controller. Remember, the list view controller communicates interactions by the user to a delegate object conforming to the ToDoItemsListViewControllerProtocol protocol we defined in *Chapter 7, Building a Table View Controller for the To-Do Items.* Follow these steps to implement this part of the setup:

1. Select the **ToDoTests** group in the project navigator and add a **Unit Test Case Class** with the name AppCoordinatorTests. Remove the two template test methods and add the @testable import ToDo import statement.

2. Now, we will make the AppCoordinator class conform to the ToDoItemsListViewControllerProtocol protocol. Add the following code to AppCoordinator.swift:

```
// AppCoordinator.swift
extension AppCoordinator:
  ToDoItemsListViewControllerProtocol {

  func selectToDoItem(_ viewController:
    UIViewController,
```

```
    item: ToDoItem) {
  }
}
```

This implementation does nothing yet. We will implement this method in the next section.

3. To write a test for assigning the delegate property of the list view controller, we need to access the list view controller in the test method. The view controller property of the AppCoordinator class is private. This means we cannot access it in the test. We could change the access level of the view controller property.

    But for educational reasons, we will do something else. We will pass a navigation controller mock into the init method of the AppCoordinator class and get the initial view controller from that.

4. Add a new Swift class to the **Doubles** group in the **ToDoTests** group and call it NavigationControllerMock. Replace the contents of that new file with the following code:

```swift
// NavigationControllerMock.swift
import UIKit


class NavigationControllerMock: UINavigationController {
  var lastPushedViewController: UIViewController?

  override func pushViewController(
    _ viewController: UIViewController,
    animated: Bool) {
    lastPushedViewController = viewController
    super.pushViewController(viewController,
      animated: animated)
  }
}
```

This subclass of the UINavigationController class stores the last pushed view controller for later inspection, and then calls the implementation of the super class.

5. Now, we can use this class in the `AppCoordinator` tests. Add the following properties to `AppCoordinatorTests`:

```
// AppCoordinatorTests.swift
var sut: AppCoordinator!
var navigationControllerMock:
NavigationControllerMock!
var window: UIWindow!
```

6. Replace the `setUpWithError` method with the following code:

```
// AppCoordinatorTests.swift
override func setUpWithError() throws {
    window = UIWindow(frame: CGRect(x: 0,
        y: 0,
        width: 200,
        height: 200))
    navigationControllerMock =
        NavigationControllerMock()
    sut = AppCoordinator(
        window: window,
        navigationController: navigationControllerMock)
}
```

In this code, we create a dummy window and an instance of `NavigationControllerMock`, and use both to initialize an instance of `AppCoordinator`.

7. What we set up for the tests, we have to clean up when the tests are finished. Replace the `tearDownWithError` method with the following code:

```
// AppCoordinatorTests.swift
override func tearDownWithError() throws {
    sut = nil
    navigationControllerMock = nil
    window = nil
}
```

8. With this preparation, we can add a test to confirm that the `start` method assigns the instance of `AppCoordinator` to the delegate of the list view controller:

```
// AppCoordinatorTests.swift
func test_start_shouldSetDelegate() throws {
  sut.start()

    let listViewController = try XCTUnwrap(
      navigationControllerMock.lastPushedViewController
      as? ToDoItemsListViewController)
    XCTAssertIdentical(
      listViewController.delegate as? AppCoordinator,
      sut)
}
```

In this test, we call the `start` method of the `AppCoordinator` instance and then assert that `sut` is assigned to the delegate property of the list view controller. We use here the `XCTAssertIdentical(_:_:)` assert function. As `AppCoordinator` is a class, we can check in the test whether the delegate is identical to `sut`. This assert function compares the pointer address of the two items, and the test passes when both references are the same. This does not work with value types because they are copied when assigned (or rather when changed).

Run the tests to confirm that this new test fails.

9. To make this test pass, add the following code to the end of the `start` method in `AppCoordinator`:

```
// AppCoordinator.swift
if let listViewController =
  viewController as? ToDoItemsListViewController {
    listViewController.delegate = self
}
```

Run the tests to confirm that this addition makes the test pass.

`ToDoItemsListViewController` shows the to-do items it gets from an instance of `ToDoItemStore`. We need to provide the list view controller with an item store when it is set up. Follow these steps to add the item store to the list view controller:

1. Add the following test to `AppCoordinatorTests`:

```
// AppCoordinatorTests.swift
func test_start_shouldAssignItemStore() throws {
  sut.start()

   let listViewController = try XCTUnwrap(
     navigationControllerMock.lastPushedViewController
     as? ToDoItemsListViewController)
   XCTAssertNotNil(listViewController.toDoItemStore)
 }
```

    In this test, we assert that the `toDoItemStore` property of the list view controller is not nil. Run the tests to confirm that this test fails.

2. Let's make this test pass. Add the following property to `AppCoordinator`:

```
// AppCoordinator.swift
let toDoItemStore: ToDoItemStore
```

3. Assign this property in the `init` method with a new instance:

```
// AppCoordinator.swift
toDoItemStore = ToDoItemStore()
```

4. Now, assign this property to the property of the list view controller within the `if let` statement of the `start` method:

```
// AppCoordinator.swift
func start() {

  navigationController.pushViewController
    (viewController,
      animated: false)
  window?.rootViewController = navigationController
```

```
    if let listViewController =
       viewController as? ToDoItemsListViewController {
      listViewController.delegate = self
      listViewController.toDoItemStore = toDoItemStore
    }
  }
```

Run the tests to confirm that all tests now pass.

The setup of the coordinator and the initial view controller is now complete. We can move on to implementing the interaction of the list view controller with the app coordinator.

When the user taps a table view cell with a to-do item, the app should navigate to the details of that item. In the following section, we will implement this feature.

Navigating to the details

We will implement the navigation within the app using the `AppCoordinator` class. Follow these steps to implement navigation to the details of to-do items:

1. Add the following test method to `AppCoordinatorTests`:

    ```
    // AppCoordinatorTests.swift
    func test_selectToDoItem_pushesDetails() throws {
      let dummyViewController = UIViewController()
      let item = ToDoItem(title: "dummy title")


      sut.selectToDoItem(dummyViewController, item: item)


      let detail = try XCTUnwrap(
        navigationControllerMock.lastPushedViewController
        as? ToDoItemDetailsViewController)
      XCTAssertEqual(detail.toDoItem, item)
    }
    ```

    In this test, we execute the `delegate` method and assert that an instance of `ToDoItemDetailsViewController` is pushed to the navigation stack, and that its `toDoItem` is the item we used in the `delegate` method call.

    Run the tests to confirm that this new test fails.

2. Replace the implementation of selectToDoItem(_:item:) with this
    implementation:

```swift
// AppCoordinator.swift
func selectToDoItem(_ viewController:
  UIViewController,
  item: ToDoItem) {

  let storyboard = UIStoryboard(name: "Main", bundle:
    nil)
  guard let next =
    storyboard.instantiateViewController(
    withIdentifier: "ToDoItemDetailsViewController")
      as? ToDoItemDetailsViewController else {
            return
          }

  next.loadViewIfNeeded()
  next.toDoItem = item

  navigationController.pushViewController(next,
    animated: true)
}
```

In this code, we instantiate an instance of ToDoItemDetailsViewController
from the storyboard and set it up with the to-do item passed into the method. Then
we push the new view controller onto the navigation stack.

Run the tests to confirm that all tests now pass again.

3. The details view controller needs a reference to toDoItemStore because the user
    can change the status of the item to done in the details view. Add the following test
    to AppCoordinatorTests:

```swift
// AppCoordinatorTests.swift
func test_selectToDoItem_shouldSetItemStore() throws {
  let dummyViewController = UIViewController()
  let item = ToDoItem(title: "dummy title")
```

```
sut.selectToDoItem(dummyViewController, item: item)

let detail = try XCTUnwrap(
  navigationControllerMock.lastPushedViewController
  as? ToDoItemDetailsViewController)
XCTAssertIdentical(
  detail.toDoItemStore as? ToDoItemStore,
  sut.toDoItemStore)
}
```

This test looks like the previous one. We only changed the assert function call to check whether the `toDoItemStore` property is identical to the `sut` property.

Run the tests to see this test failing.

4. To make this test pass, assign the `toDoItemStore` property below the line we assigned the `toDoItem` property:

```
// AppCoordinator.swift
next.loadViewIfNeeded()
next.toDoItem = item
next.toDoItemStore = toDoItemStore
```

Run the tests to confirm that all tests pass.

When the user selects a cell with a to-do item, our app now shows the details of that item on the screen. There is one feature missing. The app needs to allow the input of new to-do items. We will implement the presentation of the input view from the list view in the next section.

Navigating to a modal view

Normally, testing the presentation of a modal view controller is quite complicated. If you search how to do that on the internet, you will find that the common solutions work by swizzling the `present(_:animated:completion:)` method defined in the `UIViewController` class. Swizzling is quite complicated, and I will not show in this book how this is done.

But, because we are using the coordinator pattern for the navigation in our app, we can test the presentation without the need to swizzle any method. Still, you should look up how to swizzle methods because sometimes you don't have the option to use the coordinator pattern; for example, when there is already all the navigation code implemented and you are not allowed to change it.

Follow these steps to implement the presentation of the input view when the user chooses to add a new to-do item:

1. The app needs a button in the user interface that the user can tap to add a to-do item. When the user taps that button, the list view controller should tell its delegate about it. Add the following method definition to `ToDoItemsListViewControllerProtocol`:

    ```
    // ToDoItemsListViewController.swift
    func addToDoItem(
      _ viewController: UIViewController)
    ```

2. To make the compiler happy, add the following empty method implementation to `AppCoordinator`:

    ```
    // AppCoordinator.swift
    func addToDoItem(_ viewController: UIViewController) {
    }
    ```

3. We have another class that conforms to the `ToDoItemsListViewControllerProtocol` protocol. Add the following code to the end of the `ToDoItemsListViewControllerProtocolMock` class:

    ```
    // ToDoItemsListViewControllerProtocolMock.swift
    var addToDoItemCallCount = 0
    func addToDoItem(_ viewController: UIViewController) {
      addToDoItemCallCount += 1
    }
    ```

    The mock object counts the number of calls of the `addToDoItem(_:)` method.

4. Next, we need a view controller mock that catches the last presented view controller. Select the **Doubles** group within the **ToDoTests** group in the project navigator and add a new Swift file with the name `ViewControllerMock.swift`. Replace its content with the following code:

    ```
    // ViewControllerMock.swift
    import UIKit

    class ViewControllerMock: UIViewController {
      var lastPresented: UIViewController?
      override func present(
    ```

```
    _ viewControllerToPresent: UIViewController,
    animated flag: Bool,
    completion: (() -> Void)? = nil) {
    lastPresented = viewControllerToPresent
    super.present(viewControllerToPresent,
      animated: flag,
      completion: completion)
  }
}
```

This mock stores the presented view controller in a property for later inspection.

5. Now, we can write the test. Import SwiftUI to AppCoordinatorTests.swift and add the following test method to AppCoordinatorTests:

```
// AppCoordinatorTests.swift
func test_addToDoItem_shouldPresentInputView() throws
{
  let viewControllerMock = ViewControllerMock()

  sut.addToDoItem(viewControllerMock)

  let lastPresented = try XCTUnwrap(
    viewControllerMock.lastPresented
    as? UIHostingController<ToDoItemInputView>)
  XCTAssertIdentical(
    lastPresented.rootView.delegate as?
    AppCoordinator,
    sut)
}
```

This test calls addToDoItem(_:) and asserts that the sut variable is assigned as the delegate of the presented instance of ToDoItemInputView.

Run the tests to confirm that this new test fails.

6. To make this test pass, import SwiftUI into AppCoordinator.swift and replace the implementation of addToDoItem(_:) with the following code:

```
// AppCoordinator.swift
func addToDoItem(_ viewController: UIViewController) {
```

```
    let data = ToDoItemData()
    let next = UIHostingController(
      rootView: ToDoItemInputView(data: data,
        apiClient: APIClient(),
        delegate: self))

    viewController.present(next, animated: true)
  }
```

Xcode shows an error; we will fix this error in the next step. This code instantiates an instance of `UIHostingController` with a root view of `ToDoItemInputView`. This is how we can present a `SwiftUI` view from a `UIKit` environment.

7. To make this code compile, add the following extension to `AppCoordinator.swift`:

```
// AppCoordinator.swift
extension AppCoordinator: ToDoItemInputViewDelegate {
  func addToDoItem(with: ToDoItemData,
    coordinate: Coordinate?) {

  }
}
```

Run the tests to confirm that all tests now pass.

One part of this feature is finished. Next, we need to implement the other part in the `ToDoItemsListViewController` class.

8. Add the following test method to `ToDoItemsListViewControllerTests`:

```
// ToDoItemsListViewControllerTests.swift
func test_navigationBarButton_shouldCallDelegate()
 throws {
  let delegateMock =
  ToDoItemsListViewControllerProtocolMock()
  sut.delegate = delegateMock

  let addButton =
    sut.navigationItem.rightBarButtonItem
  let target = try XCTUnwrap(addButton?.target)
```

```
let action = try XCTUnwrap(addButton?.action)
_ = target.perform(action, with: addButton)


XCTAssertEqual(delegateMock.addToDoItemCallCount, 1)
}
```

In this test, we get the right bar button item of the sut variable and call its action on its target. This should result in a call to the addToDoItem(_:) method of the delegate.

Run the tests and confirm that this new test fails.

9. Add the following code to the end of viewDidLoad() of ToDoItemsListViewController:

```
// ToDoItemsListViewController.swift
let addItem = UIBarButtonItem(barButtonSystemItem:
    .add,
    target: self,
    action: #selector(add(_:)))
navigationItem.rightBarButtonItem = addItem
```

With this code, we add a bar button to the navigation item of the ToDoItemsListViewController instance. This results in a bar button that is added to the navigation bar of the navigation controller that hosts ToDoItemsListViewController.

10. Now, add the following method to ToDoItemsListViewController:

```
// ToDoItemsListViewController.swift
@objc func add(_ sender: UIBarButtonItem) {
}
```

For now, we let the implementation of this method empty because we want to see the test fail in the assert function call. Run the tests and confirm that the test we added last now fails in the assert call.

11. To make the test pass, add the missing code in add(_:):

```
// ToDoItemsListViewController.swift
@objc func add(_ sender: UIBarButtonItem) {
    delegate?.addToDoItem(self)
}
```

Run the tests to confirm that all tests now pass.

We already know that ToDoItemInputView calls its delegate when the user selects the **Save** button in the user interface. But, we still have to implement that the delegate calls the add(_:) method of ToDoItemStore. Take the following steps to implement this feature.

12. Add the following test to AppCoordinatorTests:

```
// AppCoordinatorTests.swift
func test_addToDoItemWith_shouldCallToDoItemStore()
 throws {
  let toDoItemData = ToDoItemData()
  toDoItemData.title = "dummy title"

  let receivedItems =
  try wait(for: sut.toDoItemStore.itemPublisher,
    afterChange: {
    sut.addToDoItem(with: toDoItemData, coordinate:
      nil)
 })

  XCTAssertEqual(receivedItems.first?.title,
    toDoItemData.title)
}
```

This test asserts that, after calling addToDoItem(with:coordinate:), now itemPublisher of the toDoItemStore property publishes the change to the stored items.

13. As we are adding a to-do item to the item store, we need to replace doToItemStore in AppCoordinator with a test store. Otherwise, the test could fail because of items added to the store in other tests or while we test the app on the simulator.

14. Replace the init method of the AppCoordinator class with the following implementation:

```
// AppCoordinator.swift
init(window: UIWindow?,
  navigationController: UINavigationController =
    UINavigationController(),
```

```
          toDoItemStore: ToDoItemStore = ToDoItemStore()) {

    self.window = window
    self.navigationController = navigationController
    self.toDoItemStore = toDoItemStore

    let storyboard = UIStoryboard(name: "Main", bundle:
      nil)
    viewController =
      storyboard.instantiateViewController(
      withIdentifier: "ToDoItemsListViewController")
  }
```

Here, we have added the `toDoItemStore` parameter to the method and we use that parameter to set the `toDoItemStore` property used in the `AppCoordinator` class.

15. So, we can use a test store when setting up `sut` in `setUpWithError`:

```
// AppCoordinatorTests.swift
override func setUpWithError() throws {
  window = UIWindow(frame: CGRect(x: 0,
    y: 0,
    width: 200,
    height: 200))
  navigationControllerMock =
    NavigationControllerMock()
  sut = AppCoordinator(
    window: window,
    navigationController: navigationControllerMock,
    toDoItemStore: ToDoItemStore(fileName:
      "dummy_store"))
}
```

16. To delete the item store when the test is finished, add the following code to the end of `tearDownWithError` of `AppCoordinatorTests`:

```swift
// AppCoordinatorTests.swift
let url = FileManager.default
  .documentsURL(name: "dummy_store")
try? FileManager.default.removeItem(at: url)
```

This code should look familiar, as we already used it in `ToDoItemStoreTests`.

Run the tests to confirm that the new test fails.

17. Make the test pass with the following implementation of `addToDoItem(with:coordinate:)`:

```swift
// AppCoordinator.swift
func addToDoItem(with item: ToDoItemData,
  coordinate: Coordinate?) {
  let location = Location(name: item.locationName,
    coordinate: coordinate)

  let toDoItem = ToDoItem(
    title: item.title,
    itemDescription: item.itemDescription,
    timestamp: item.date.timeIntervalSince1970,
    location: location)

  toDoItemStore.add(toDoItem)
}
```

Note that we added an internal parameter name of `item` for the first parameter of that method.

In this code, we create an instance of `ToDoItem` from the `ToDoItemData` structure. Then, we call the `add(_:)` method of `toDoItemStore`.

Run the tests to confirm that this change makes all tests pass again.

For now, we are done with the implementation. Let's make the app work in the simulator and see whether we missed something.

Adding missing parts

First, let's run the app for the first time to see where we are.

The app starts with a blank screen with just one plus (+) button in the upper-right corner.

Figure 11.2 – The initial view of our app

So, there is work to do here. But, let's move on and tap the plus (+) button. We are presented with the input view. We can add data for the item and tap the **Save** button.

Figure 11.3 – The input view of our app

But, when we tap the **Save** button, nothing happens. Dismiss the view by swiping down, and see whether the item was added. Something changed. There is a blank table view cell visible in the middle of the screen.

Figure 11.4 – A blank table view cell. Where is the to-do item?

When you tap the blank table view cell, the detail view is pushed onto the screen.

Figure 11.5 – The details of the to-do item. But, where is the due date?

Okay, we have some work to do. Let's go back to Xcode and fix some problems.

Making the cells visible

The table view doesn't show the information of the to-do items. The reason is, we didn't add constraints to the views when we added the labels. This was on purpose because I believe you should not write unit tests to test the position and size of interface elements. UI tests of snapshot tests are a better tool for these kinds of tests.

Follow these steps to fix the layout of the cells and the table view:

1. Open `Main.storyboard` in **Interface Builder** and select the table view in **To Do Items List View Controller Scene**. Then, select the **Add New Constraints** button in the lower-right corner of **Interface Builder**. Set the top, leading, trailing, and bottom constraints to `0` and click **Add 4 Constraints**.

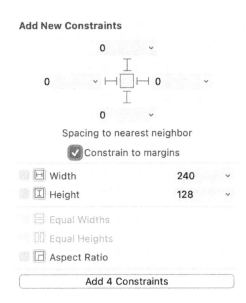

Figure 11.6 – The constraints for the table view

2. Next, go to `ToDoItemCell`, and replace the `init` method with the following implementation:

```
// ToDoItemCell.swift
override init(style: UITableViewCell.CellStyle,
    reuseIdentifier: String?) {
    titleLabel = UILabel()

    dateLabel = UILabel()
    dateLabel.textAlignment = .right

    locationLabel = UILabel()

    let titleLocation = UIStackView(
```

```
      arrangedSubviews: [titleLabel, locationLabel])
    titleLocation.axis = .vertical

    let stackView = UIStackView(
      arrangedSubviews: [titleLocation, dateLabel])
    stackView
      .translatesAutoresizingMaskIntoConstraints = false

    super.init(style: style,
      reuseIdentifier: reuseIdentifier)

    contentView.addSubview(stackView)

    NSLayoutConstraint.activate([
      stackView.topAnchor.constraint(
        equalTo: contentView.topAnchor, constant: 5),
      stackView.leadingAnchor.constraint(
        equalTo: contentView.leadingAnchor, constant: 16),
      stackView.bottomAnchor.constraint(
        equalTo: contentView.bottomAnchor, constant: -5),
      stackView.trailingAnchor.constraint(
        equalTo: contentView.trailingAnchor, constant: -
        16),
    ])
  }
```

We use `UIStackView` instances to lay out the elements. Run the tests to confirm that we didn't break anything. Then, run the app again on the simulator.

It looks better, but the due date is still missing in the table view cell. The reason is that we didn't set up the `dateFormatter` instance currently. We found a bug. Whenever we find a bug, we should try to write a test that fails because of that bug. Then, we should make the test pass by fixing the bug.

3. Add the following test method to `ToDoItemsListViewControllerTests`:

```
// ToDoItemsListViewControllerTests.swift
func test_dateFormatter_shouldNotBeNone() {
  XCTAssertNotEqual(sut.dateFormatter.dateStyle,
```

```
        .none)
    }
```

Note that the XCTAssertNotEqual assert function does the opposite of the XCTAssertEqual function. It passes when the two values are not equal.

Run the tests to see this test failing.

4. To make this test pass and the bug disappear, add these lines to viewDidLoad below the super.viewDidLoad() line:

```
// ToDoItemsListViewController.swift
super.viewDidLoad()

dateFormatter.dateStyle = .short
```

5. Run the tests to confirm that this makes the test green. Then, run the app on the simulator. Woohoo! We fixed our first bug with the help of TDD. This is a milestone. We are now sure that this bug won't come back as long as this test is run regularly.

Next, we need to fix the bug that the input view is not dismissed when the user taps the **Save** button.

Dismissing the input view

Again, we have a bug. Let's see whether we can write a test for that bug. Follow these steps to fix the bug:

1. The navigation controller mock should register if dismiss(animated:completion:) got called. This way, we can make sure that it is called when a new item is added. Add the following code to NavigationControllerMock:

```
// NavigationControllerMock.swift
var dismissCallCount = 0
override func dismiss(animated flag: Bool,
    completion: (() -> Void)? = nil) {
    dismissCallCount += 1
    super.dismiss(animated: flag,
        completion: completion)
}
```

This code counts the times dismiss(animated:completion:) got called.

2. Add the following test method to `AppCoordinatorTests`:

```
// AppCoordinatorTests.swift
func test_addToDoItemWith_shouldDismissInput() {
    let toDoItemData = ToDoItemData()
    toDoItemData.title = "dummy title"

    sut.addToDoItem(with: toDoItemData,
        coordinate: nil)

    XCTAssertEqual(
        navigationControllerMock.dismissCallCount, 1)
}
```

Run the tests to see this test failing.

3. Add the following code to the end of `addToDoItem(with:coordinate:)`:

```
// AppCoordinatorTests.swift
navigationController.dismiss(animated: true)
```

Run the tests to confirm that this code makes all tests pass again. Then, run the app and add a new to-do item.

We fixed another bug using TDD.

Next, let's fix the bug in the details that the due date isn't shown.

Making the due date visible in the details

The reason that the date is not shown in the details is the same as for the table view cell. The date formatter isn't set up correctly. You already know how to write a test for this. Write the test and make sure that the test fails.

To make the test pass and, therefore, fix the bug, you can use this definition of the `dateFormatter` property:

```
// ToDoItemDetailsViewController.swift
let dateFormatter: DateFormatter = {
    let formatter = DateFormatter()
    formatter.dateStyle = .short
    return formatter
}()
```

This should make your test pass.

Run the app again, and play around with it. You might realize some more bugs. Here is what I found:

- When the user taps the **Done** button in the details, the app should pop back to the list of to-do items.

- The section headers are missing in the table view. The done items are correctly moved to the second section, but it's not visible in the user interface that there are several sections.

- When the user marks the first item done, the order in the table view changes. If the user then selects the first item in the table view, the details for the other item are shown.

- The cell stays selected even after the user came back from the details.

- The debug console shows a warning that the table view was told to lay out the cells when it is not visible.

We sure found some more bugs.

In the following sections, we will fix only the third and the fifth bug in this list. The other bugs are left as an exercise for you. If you get stuck, have a look at the code for this chapter on GitHub.

Fixing the wrong item being selected

Again, let's try to write a test for this bug before we try to fix it. Follow these steps to fix that bug:

1. The problem is that we set up the sections when we create the snapshot for the diffable data source, but we ignore the section when the user selects a table view row. We can change the `test_didSelectCellAt_shouldCallDelegate` method to check for this error. Replace the implementation of that test method with the following code:

```
// ToDoItemsListViewControllerTests.swift
func test_didSelectCellAt_shouldCallDelegate() throws
  {
    let delegateMock =
      ToDoItemsListViewControllerProtocolMock()
    sut.delegate = delegateMock
    var doneItem = ToDoItem(title: "done item")
```

```
doneItem.done = true
let toDoItem = ToDoItem(title: "to-do item")
toDoItemStoreMock.itemPublisher
    .send([doneItem, toDoItem])
let tableView = try XCTUnwrap(sut.tableView)

let indexPath = IndexPath(row: 0, section: 0)
tableView.delegate?.tableView?(
    tableView,
    didSelectRowAt: indexPath)

XCTAssertEqual(
    delegateMock.selectToDoItemReceivedArguments?.item,
    toDoItem)
}
```

We change the test to use two items, one done item and one item that is not done yet.

Run the tests to see this test failing.

2. To make the test pass and thus fix the bug, replace the implementation of `tableView(_:didSelectRowAt:)` with the following code:

```
// ToDoItemsListViewController.swift
func tableView(_ tableView: UITableView,
    didSelectRowAt indexPath: IndexPath) {

    let item: ToDoItem
    switch indexPath.section {
    case 0:
        let filteredItems = items.filter({ false ==
            $0.done })
        item = filteredItems[indexPath.row]
    default:
        let filteredItems = items.filter({ true ==
            $0.done })
        item = filteredItems[indexPath.row]

    }
```

```
        delegate?.selectToDoItem(self, item: item)
    }
```

In this implementation, we respect the two sections and choose the item to be shown accordingly.

Run all tests to confirm that all tests now pass.

And, with this last bug fixed, we are done with the first simple version of our little app that we created using TDD.

Fixing the layout of the table view

The problem here is that we use the `Combine` framework to update the table view. When the user taps the **Done** button in the details, `doToItemStore` updates its items and tells the table view about it. This results in an update of the table view when it is not visible on the screen. This is easy to fix and we don't even need a test for this. Add the following code to `ToDoItemsListViewController`:

```
// ToDoItemsListViewController.swift
override func viewDidAppear(_ animated: Bool) {
  super.viewDidAppear(animated)

  token = toDoItemStore?.itemPublisher
    .sink(receiveValue: { [weak self] items in
      self?.items = items
      self?.update(with: items)
    })
}

override func viewWillDisappear(_ animated: Bool) {
  super.viewWillDisappear(animated)

  token?.cancel()
}
```

When the view with the table view disappears, we unsubscribe from `itemsPublisher`. When the view appears on the screen, we subscribe again. Run the app again in the simulator and have a look at the console to see whether the message is gone.

Summary

In this final chapter, we have implemented the navigation between the different views of our app. We have learned how to test pushing view controllers onto a navigation stack and how we can test whether a view got presented modally.

With navigation implemented, we started the app on the simulator and found and fixed bugs. We figured out that TDD even helps when fixing bugs. By writing first a failing test for that bug and then making the test pass, we ensured that this bug won't hurt us in the future of our app.

With the skills you gained in this chapter, you will be able to implement and test the navigation of an app using the coordinator pattern. And, you are now able to write tests for bugs and fix the bug by making the test pass.

Congratulations, you reached the end of this book! My hope is that this book is the beginning of your journey to becoming a test-driven developer. You learned how to test Combine code and write tests for view controllers and views, table views, and even SwiftUI code. I believe this is a good foundation for your next steps. Try to add tests to your existing projects and talk to your colleagues about the advantages and disadvantages of unit tests and TDD. Find your own testing style.

Most importantly, have fun!

Exercises

1. Fix the bugs you found while testing the app on the simulator.

2. Add the feature that the user can check to-do items in the list of all to-do items.

3. Write a review for this book on Amazon.

Index

Other Books You May Enjoy

If you enjoyed this book, you may be interested in these other books by Packt:

SwiftUI Cookbook

Giordano Scalzo , Edgar Nzokwe

ISBN: 978-1-80323-445-8

- Explore various layout presentations in SwiftUI such as HStack, VStack, LazyHStack, and LazyVGrid
- Create widgets to quickly display relevant content at glance
- Get up to speed with drawings in SwiftUI using built-in shapes, custom paths, and polygons
- Discover modern animation and transition techniques in SwiftUI
- Add user authentication using Firebase and Sign in with Apple
- Manage concurrency with Combine and async/await in SwiftUI
- Solve the most common SwiftUI problems, such as integrating a MapKit map, unit testing, snapshot testing, and previewing layouts

SwiftUI Projects

Craig Clayton

ISBN: 978-1-83921-466-0

- Understand the basics of SwiftUI by building an app with watchOS
- Work with UI elements such as text, lists, and buttons
- Create a video player in UIKit and import it into SwiftUI
- Discover how to leverage an API and parse JSON in your app using Combine
- Structure your app to use Combine and state-driven features
- Create flexible layouts on iPad

Packt is searching for authors like you

If you're interested in becoming an author for Packt, please visit `authors.packtpub.com` and apply today. We have worked with thousands of developers and tech professionals, just like you, to help them share their insight with the global tech community. You can make a general application, apply for a specific hot topic that we are recruiting an author for, or submit your own idea.

Hi!

I am Dominik Hauser, author of *Test-Driven iOS Development with Swift* Fourth Edition. I really hope you enjoyed reading this book and found it useful for increasing your productivity and efficiency in iOS development.

It would really help me (and other potential readers!) if you could leave a review on Amazon sharing your thoughts on *Test-Driven iOS Development with Swift* Fourth Edition.

Go to the link below or scan the QR code to leave your review:

`https://packt.link/r/180323248X`

Your review will help me to understand what's worked well in this book, and what could be improved upon for future editions, so it really is appreciated.

Best Wishes,

D. Hauser

Made in the USA
Las Vegas, NV
20 December 2022

63702035R00155